Bradshaw's Guide to
D.I.Y.
House Buying, Selling and Conveyancing

Joseph Bradshaw, B.A.

Castle Books

LEAMINGTON SPA

©
Joseph Bradshaw
1980
ISBN: 09507170 0 2

2nd Impression
1981

2nd Edition
1983
reprinted 1983 (twice)
ISBN: 09507170 5 3
Hardback ISBN: 09507170 6 1

By the same author:

Bradshaw's Guide to House Conveyancing for Sitting Tenants
ISBN: 09507170 1 0

Bradshaw's Guide to Conveyancing by Way of Gift or Inheritance
ISBN: 09507170 2 9

Bradshaw's Guide to Marketing Your House
ISBN: 09507170 4 5

Printed and bound by Eyre and Spottiswoode Ltd,
Thanet Press, Margate

Castle Books, 1 Blackdown, Leamington Spa CV32 6RA.

CONTENTS

Acknowledgements   v

Preface to Second Edition   vi

Introduction   vii

1. **Sell First or Buy First?**   1
2. **Putting Your House on the Market**   4
3. **Estate Agents**   10
4. **Viewing**   19
5. **New Houses**   36
6. **Mortgages**   40
7. **Contracts**   47
8. **Gazumping**   56
9. **The Registers**   61
10. **Doing Your Own Conveyance**   77
11. **Doing the Sale and Purchase of a Registered House**   86
12. **Doing the Sale and Purchase of an Unregistered House**   121
13. **Selling Leasehold Property**   147
14. **Matrimonal Homes**   150
15. **Did You Know?**   156

APPENDIX I: Land Registry Addresses   162

Index   166

Glossary   174

Buying at Auction   176

Flow diagrams   178

Acknowledgements

I am grateful to all those members of the public who trusted me to help and guide them through their housing problems. They, in putting their questions and thus demonstrating the gaps in their knowledge and confidence alerted me to the needs of owner occupiers, who are savers, triers, plotters, planners — in short, people who will do what they can for themselves. It was in consideration of the needs of these splendid people that I felt justified in adding to the flow of advice that assails them, but which, sad to say, usually concludes with the costly advice......go to a professional. You won't find any of that here!

Mr. K. W. Clark F S V A of Daltons, Leeds, drawing on over a quarter of a century's experience and knowledge, gave me invaluable advice and criticism of the chapters about Estates Agents, Mortgages and Viewing. Chapters 10 to 15 were scrutinised by a Legal Executive who for obvious reasons prefers to remain anonymous for the next few years.

The Controller of Her Majesty's Stationery Office gave permission to reproduce the Land Registry forms, and the Times Newspaper gave permission to reproduce what their writer Roger Berthoud called 'the Deterding diatribe.'

Above all I thank my wife Margaret who has not only put up with me and my obsession while writing this book, but also went through the script putting in the dots and commas. She even put in some of the funnies. Any claim that the book has to any kind of readability or literary merit is all hers.

While I thank all those who have contributed down the years to my stock of knowledge and experience in the property field, and those who have helped me with this book, I accept all the responsibility. I will also be pleased to accept any anecdotes or comments from recruits this book makes to the growing band of D.I.Y. conveyancers.

Preface to the Second Edition

In the two years since the first edition of this Bradshaw's Guide I have received hundreds of the most heart-warming letters from readers and users. I thank them all. Goodness knows how much money has been saved by all the people who have sold and bought their houses for themselves using these pages.

A glossary, a sample conveyance, a key to the abominable word abbreviations used by lawyers, and a few words about auctions and why solicitors are nice to DIY conveyancers were among the ideas readers offered for this edition. Where within the format it has been possible to add them it has been done. References to some of the forms are scattered throughout the book and as it makes for tedious reading when information is repeated, the index has been extended as an aid to navigation from one reference to the next.

I also thank both the barrister and legal executive who gave this updated edition the once-over for me.

Saving money has not been the exclusive attraction of this book. Those who do no more than read it, and get the message, find it valuable as an aid to understanding what is involved, particularly in conveyancing. As a pleasant reward for their trouble they find professionals keep their fees within reasonable limits once they realise that they have a knowledgeable client on their hands.

Castle Books forms service has proved a useful two-way communicator enabling me to have distributed with the packs of forms up-dating bulletins showing the latest changes affecting conveyancing. I appreciate what I have heard from readers, look forward to more, and assure one and all that I have never heard of a DIY conveyancer making a mess of it. Evidently they always get it right, and when you have read the book I hope you will agree it would be difficult to do otherwise.

Joseph Bradshaw 1983

As the Solicitors' Law Stationery Society has now agreed to sell forms and contracts to the public, Castle Books' forms service is no longer necessary and has been discontinued.

J.B. September 1983

Introduction

This is the age of Do It Yourself. From painting and decorating to car maintenance, people are having a go themselves. And it isn't only practical things that are being tackled.

A few years ago the technicalities for obtaining a divorce were simplified and a little later the government withdrew the provision of legal aid for parties to divorces which were not defended. The increasing popularity of divorce and the bankrupting nature of solicitors' fees for doing the transaction have between them produced thousands of do-it-yourself divorcees who have, for less than £30 a pair, done their own divorces, and saved themselves over £300 by expending a little time and effort. Moreover, during the process of doing their own divorces people have found that what hitherto they thought was a thoroughly legal process is only judicial insofar as a judge has to give a nod over their papers, and all the rest is simply an administrative matter.

In this book, I hope to show that housing transactions have even less of the law about them than divorce actions. Nowadays, transferring a house from one owner to another is done, in most of England and Wales, by filling in simple forms — that is the legal side of it. The bit that can be complicated is when you are using the sale monies from one house to pay for the purchase of another. But that is not a legal problem, it is a business transaction. You don't hare off to a fully-trained legal man when you are trading up-market from a Bentley to a Rolls; settling the HP on one and taking out a new loan on the other. You no more need to know the Law of Property and Mortgages Acts inside out when you buy a house than you need to know the Road Traffic and Consumer Credit Acts when buying or selling a car. Whether it is a house or car that is being dealt with you need to know about honesty and fair dealing and if you meet up with someone who sells you an unroadworthy car or seriously misrepresents a property to you, the laws are there to punish the offender; it is then that you really need a lawyer — a good one.

Just because wrongdoers can be punished under Acts of Parliament, this does not mean to say you should not be prudent within your competence. If you are considering buying a car that has done a fair mileage, you put it through some stringent tests, and if you are not sure about it, but still interested, at a price, you can get a qualified mechanic to give you a report on it. If you want to make sure there is no Hire Purchase on it, go to the local Citizens' Advice Bureau (don't ring, there's a form to fill in) and for little more than the cost of a stamp they will check it out for you. So there you are, the legal owner of a bigger and better car, and you need know no more law at the end of the transaction than at the beginning. But look at what you have accomplished: you have satisfied yourself that the car is what it is cracked up to be and checked that the person offering it for sale owns (has good title to) it. "Ah!", you say, "houses are not like cars. Surely it's more complicated, and doesn't the rule *caveat emptor* (let the buyer beware) apply in full force to a housing transaction? Isn't the whole business a splendid opportunity for scoundrels to practice their wicked ways?".

My answer is: certainly houses are not like cars. Cars can be stolen; repainted; engine and number plates swapped. You can't very well shift a whole house. As for let the buyer beware, in its application to housing it is, in the main, a reference to the purchaser making sure that the vendor has good title (can prove he owns and has the power to sell) and as you will learn from these pages, you obtain this assurance by sending a simple form and £2.25p (1980) to the Land Registry*. Another dreadful thing that can happen is that you don't get full vacant possession when you have paid over your money. No law, no lawyer, can save you from this calamity unless you yourself follow the instruction given in this book. No solicitor has a better method than that given here; and if, when you last bought a house, any precautions were taken to make sure that you did get vacant possession before the money was handed over (and vice versa when you sold) the odds are that it was you who did the legwork. Solicitors rely on the general law, together with the basic honesty of the absolute majority of house-owners on these practical points. On the legal point of proving ownership, where the ownership is registered, they rely on the state-backed guarantee to be obtained from Her Majesty's Registry Office; I invite you to do the same.

H. M. Land Registry was established at the end of the nineteenth century, the Land Transfer Act which set it up having finally made its way through Parliament after centuries of attempts had failed. If you read what the sponsors of the Act had to say in its support you will see that they intended to make dealing in land as simple as dealing in, to use their nineteenth century words, "stock and chattels". To that end the Land Registry was established and of course someone

---

*Forms — Some are obtainable from Her Majesty's Stationery Office — others from OYEZ publishers, and others from Inland Revenue Stamp Office.

*Fee 1983: £3.

has to pay its upkeep. Who better than those who benefit — the Public? Today, the buyer of the average house, pays
about £40* to the Registry — but who has had the dealing
simplified for him? — the Lawyer.

It is ironic that an Act passed nearly a century ago to
benefit the general public at a time when most people had
left school at eleven years of age or earlier has been made to
appear so complicated that the vast majority of house buyers
and sellers who will have had at least eleven years of schooling
are being persuaded to pay solicitors to do something they
could well do for themselves. It tells us something, either
about our education system or about the lawyer's propaganda
machine, I think it is the latter. Indeed, the propaganda
is so effective it has even convinced lawyers themselves that
they really are protecting their clients from a thousand and
one things that can go wrong.

I have done my own little survey. I put this question,
'What do you think a solicitor does for you that you could not
do for yourself?" Invariably the answer is "All those searches".
This answer is usually spoken with such reverential awe it
seems that ordinary trusting people have come to believe that
everytime they buy a house their solicitor has worked his way
through reference after reference, file after file, and book
after book in office after office and cellar after cellar, emerging
with the scrolls into the light of day, covered in dust and with a
cold wet towel round his head, cursing his father for not
letting him work on a car-production line to earn his living.

In reality, the searching consists in sending off a few
forms, which have ready-printed questions, to the authorities
who answer them for you. If you really find this difficult to
believe, at least have a look at the said forms. Unfortunately
most of them are copyright, and though that does not stop
you using them (they have to be paid for, so the copyright
holders are glad to sell) it does stop unauthorised publica-
tion, so we can't show them here. When you do see these forms
I am sure you will agree that of all the forms you have ever had
the misfortune to struggle with, those used in housing transactions suffer least from officialese and gobble-de-gook. If you
have already bought or sold a house you will have found that

*1983: £60

the only thing about the whole transaction which struck you as truly professional was the sheer size of the bill at the end of it. It doesn't matter whether your conveyance was done by a qualified solicitor or a clerk in his office who had one or two 'O' levels, you got the same job done and the same breath-taking bill.

Another thing that really seemed to puzzle the respondents to my little survey was — how did one manage to use the money from the sale of one house for the purchase of another when it is well known that one has to actually move out before one will be paid. As you will learn it can be done when you can get all the parties together at the same time. But where that is not possible it is done by the simple expedient of a bridging loan from your bank. The interest is at 3% over base rate, so on £20,000 the charge at 20% is a mere £10.46p per day with a minimum of £15 plus a fee of £2 or £3. Many is the vendor-cum-purchaser who has had to pay bridging loan charges in addition to solicitors' fees. When you do your own conveyancing at least you make sure that the days are not ticking away and your costs rising.

Conveyancing can appear to be very lucrative for solicitors. Of course like everybody else they have big expenses nowadays. Office rents are not cheap, typists demand a living wage; they also require central heating and are not prepared to type on any old machine. Solicitors have also been known to defend the high cost of conveyancing on the ground that it subsidises the pitifully low rates of pay they receive for work in some criminal courts. Lord Longford will no doubt think that a reasonable arrangement; he and his côterie will read no further. Whether solicitors, given their costly overheads, are doing conveyances as cheaply as they could, the fact remains that house owners are increasingly coming to the conclusion that lawyers' shops are situate in a market they cannot afford to patronise. Indeed, many people with young growing families are aching to move house but are deterred by the high costs.

Over the years I have, as a property owner, conveyed dozens of properties for myself — nothing has ever gone wrong. Never have I regretted my action, and neither have I ever met any other do-it-yourself conveyancer who has any such regrets. Sorting out problems that house buyers and sellers have brought to me at the Citizens' Advice Bureau has convinced me that it would have been better for many of them had they tackled the job themselves from the beginning.

Transferring property is nowhere near as difficult as it has been made out to be, but that does not mean to say that the technical work can be done by a two-year-old chimpanzee suffering from brain damage. If in a few of the pages that follow it seems rather complicated, take courage and keep going, remembering it's all new to you. It might even be shock that is stopping your brain functioning; shock at the simplicity, and shame as you realise how in the past you have been so easily persuaded that it was all so fantastically difficult.

Though it is hoped that the book makes an interesting and useful read in itself, it is intended to be kept at the D.I.Y. conveyancer's elbow for reference as he picks his way through buying and selling and conveyancing for himself.

On the way he will notice that strategies and tactics are given so that purchasers pay less and vendors get more. This inherent paradox can only make life more interesting all round where both vendor and purchaser have invested in the book. So if you spot from your opposite number's tactics that he is a fellow reader, keep the knowledge to yourself, simply turn back to the book and check up on how to cope with him. Why let the professionals have all the fun? — do the job yourself and take a pride in it!

1. Sell First
or Buy First?

If you have never bought a house before then the question answers itself. But if you are an owner who needs to move to a larger or smaller house, or needs to get away from the neighbours or in-laws, or needs to raise some money by buying a cheaper house, which way round you work is crucial. The decision has to be made in the light of both your personal needs and resources, and the general state of the housing market at the time.

You can, of course, go out viewing properties, and when you see one that suits you, say "Yes, I will buy this when I have sold my own." And you might drag the vendors on for ages while you screw the last penny out of your sale. On the other hand, the vendor of your dream property may have read this book too, and the answer will be "I'll give you x number of weeks." How many times have you heard of "chains" breaking down? How many times have you seen the silly "sold subject to contract" slips pasted onto and then taken off "For Sale" boards? Greed, slipshod estate agents and lawyers' bad timing are the usual causes.

Since the mid nineteen-thirties there has been a drift upwards in prices, but the movement goes in fits and starts: so spot the rising market and you can safely buy first, and be pretty sure of selling your own house swiftly and profitably. You can always tell when the housing market has reached its bottom and is about to rise. Similarly, you get a very clear signal that a boom is within six months or so of petering out: *The mass media will tell you.* When they make headlines out of the fact that young people are being priced out of the market, and when they have stories about people making fortunes in a few years out of houses, the market is at the top. Nevertheless, so as not to miss the bus, new buyers join in, and so keep the pot boiling a little longer. But the bus was just about to pull up at a compulsory stop. On the other hand, when, on your telly, you see a lugubrious man standing in front of his "For Sale" board, which has obviously taken root, and he tells you that he has not had sign, sound nor smell of a viewer for over eighteen months, then the market is about to pick up. If you can spot these market changes you will know what to do.

Unless what you want to buy is unique, buy first in a rising market, and sell first at the top of the market, or when it has started to fall. But for goodness sake, unless you have the purchase money in the bank, follow the general rule and don't sign a contract to buy unless you have already got a signed contract from your own purchaser. Now that is a general rule, and rules, like pie-crusts, were made to be broken, so when you come to Chap. 8 I will show you how to protect yourself from being gazumped if you feel you are buying for thousands less than the real worth, and your only problem is that you have not yet got a purchaser signed up for your own house.

The usual deposit paid on signing contracts is 10% but in these days of 95% mortgages, one can always try paying only 5%. Vendors expect something to be paid as a sign of good faith when an agreement has been reached subject to contract, and usually £100 or £200 is sufficient. What it is sufficient for I'll never know because at any time before a binding contract is signed, either party for any or no reason can withdraw. The vendor can pay the deposit back, the purchaser can demand the return of his deposit. But people seem to like to play this game, encouraged by estate agents and solicitors. Hence gazumping and chains "collapsing".

However, if you are selling at, say, £20,000 and get £2,000 out of your purchaser on exchanging signed contracts, you on the same day, can safely pay £2,000 deposit on your purchase, and that link of the chain is closed. If the house you are buying is, say, £40,000, try the 5%, which is £2,000, but if more is demanded and the sum is not negotiable, go to the bank. You have a copper-bottomed contract that is about to bring you £20,000, less what it costs to pay off your mortgage, so you are not really poverty-stricken. The bank will always help people who want money but don't really need it. But again, get it clear what the terms are, and make sure you can't do better at another bank or through your estate agent. Well-secured bridging loans are good business so be fair and let them all have a chance.

2. Putting Your House
on the Market

As soon as you decide to sell and have given notice of your intention to your Building Society, get rid of the junk as quickly as the dustbin men will take it away. Bottles, jars, containers of all sorts that you never had time to fill with home-made preserves. Magazines and newspapers you intended to read again and never did. Offcuts of material from cotton to chipboard that you were sure would come in useful, together with the bent nails and screws which never did either. The clothes you hoped would come back into fashion. Let the lot go. Junk expands to fill the available space. It is astounding how we all imagine that a house or garden which is neat, tidy and well-kept, will easily remain so. Viewers seem to think so too. A mucky house in a tatty garden has to be sold muck cheap. So, tidy up. It makes the happy home look more spacious and valuable immediately you have done so.

Having been fairly ruthless, look at what's left and decide

what you will take with you and what you can leave for the purchasers. If all vendors would only leave the curtain rails and all but the most costly light fittings, it would be a mercy to all. But nobody seems to know exactly what should be left and what can be taken; what constitutes a fixture and what a fitting. Appealing to common sense is in fact, in this case, a better guide than appealing to the law, and infinitely cheaper.

Fixtures, by custom, seem to include all permanencies and semi-permanencies that one can't simply walk up to, pick up and walk away with. Buildings, lawns, rose bushes and television aerials are fixtures. You can put the lamp shade under your arm and walk away with it, but the light switch is a different matter. It is the bits and pieces other than what are obvious parts of the house (such as the doors) and what are obviously not part of the house (such as the carpets) which cause the trouble. Situations where it's not strictly breach of contract to remove an item but would be a breach of good faith to do so should be avoided. All this is not to say that you simply cannot take the doors. Of course you can — but you must make it clear to the purchaser that you so intend, because anyone can reasonably assume that a door is a fixture and part of the house. Make up your mind about the things which might just look, to someone else, like a fixture or fitting (the cooker, for instance) and decide what you intend taking and what you intend leaving.

Decide what you would like to sell (curtains, carpets, etc.). Make a list. In fact, make a few, ready for the rush of viewers you can expect if you are a sensible vendor who has a neat and tidy house, sensibly advertised at a sensible price.

Since the day you bought your house, I take it that you, like most proud owners, have taken a lively interest in the property for sale in your district. You will have noted houses such as your own that were advertised for more money than you gave, and ignored those that looked cheaper. You did right, at the time it made you feel pounds better. The psychologists call this process 'cognitive dissonance'. Similarly, you will have seen houses for sale in the class and district that you wished to move to, but in this case, you will have noted the cheaper ones and tried to ignore the dearer. After all, you are the clever buyer and seller, aren't you, but do give others credit for having done the same. Realise also that you have only seen the figures that vendors would like for their properties and not in fact what they get. So bear this in mind when deciding the price at which to put your own house on the market. A house for which a vendor has asked way above the odds does not sell. It becomes a drug on the market, even when reduced to below market price. Your first viewers are your best viewers, but remember, you only need one buyer.

So when you have tidied up and decided your price, whether to call in an estate agent depends on your experience of, and with, estate agents. If you know an agent who will treat the sale of your house as if it were his own — get him on the job, quick. Such a man will not only take all the worry off your shoulders, but will more than cover the cost of his commission in the price he gets and the money he saves you on advertising. The qualities of such an estate agent will be discussed later, but if you know of no such paragon, then have a go yourself.

Your aim is to let as many people as possible know that you are selling. The quickest way is to put a board in the garden. If you haven't got one and don't know where to borrow one, make a good one — you, your friends, relatives and neighbours are bound to need it again.

Having lived in the area for a few years you will know which newspapers carry most of the property sale advertisements. The local agents have been testing the papers for years and know which pulls best, so follow their lead. But be careful not to follow the agents in the wording of your advertisement.

Everbody understands that agents are allowed their "puffs" in adverts, and it is quite amazing how far they can go without looking silly. However, where they can get away with "bijou residence of great charm" or "tastefully" this and "uniquely" that, you are at risk of looking silly in the eyes of your friends, and what is worse, in the eyes of prospective purchasers. There are some writers who would try to put the wind up you by cautioning you to heed the Trades Description Acts. I won't bother. After all, trying to answer the question as to what is tasteful, delightful, charming or any other descriptive word or phrase is as absurd as trying to answer the question "How long is a piece of string?".

A sensible advertisement for the private vendor simply states the facts of what he has to sell, gives the asking price and arrangements for viewing. Do not say too much. Do not forget that it was curiosity which killed the cat. Remember the tale of the woman who refused to view any house unless it had a walk-in pantry. Now, the same woman had always considered that any house which sported a well-established wistaria was really superior. So when she received particulars of a house and they were silent on the question of pantry, she viewed, and bought. There was no pantry, but, not only was there a wistaria, but it was in full bloom. Also remember that there may be people who cannot stand the sight, colour or smell of wistaria and wouldn't view if they knew your house sported one, but will be so impressed by the rest of the residence, they will make digging out the wistaria their first gardening job. So least said, soonest mended.

Your first task is to get the viewers. If the house you have for sale looks good enough to grace a calendar or chocolate box lid, by all means put a photograph of it in the newspapers. Otherwise, it seems best to use the space attractively by having plenty of white space surrounding the black lettering of the advert. I know there has been a trend in recent years for estate agents to publish photos of *all* their wares. But I also know that one could be forgiven for thinking that many of these photos were intended to put prospective buyers off from viewing, rather than the reverse.

If people knock on the door in response to seeing the board in your garden, and you are not alone in the house, let them in. Only if the most embarrassing scene is being enacted within should you ask them to come back later. From first to last remember that doubtless this is your most prizeable possession that you are trying to sell. You must be prepared to work at it and accept some inconvenience. You only need one buyer and she may well be the lady standing before your very eyes. It might cost you another fifty pounds in advertising before you get another viewer, so a bird on the doorstep can be worth two in the bush.

If people ring up for an appointment to view remember the walk-in pantry lady, and say as little as possible over the phone. Do not worry too much about the problem of time-wasters. They might arrive at the same time as a genuine prospect, and the so-called time-waster might just jerk the prospect into action. Most people tend to want what others want — it confirms their own good judgement.

When the viewers come in daylight make sure the curtains are drawn well back. Have doors onto landings and passages open to let light in. It all makes a house look more airy and spacious. If there is more than one of you at home when the viewers arrive by appointment, decide beforehand who is to lead the conducted tour, leaving the others seated very comfortably in the lounge.

Those who are light-fingered work to the four A's; they will steal anything from anybody, anywhere, anytime. So don't leave pocketable things around. Don't actually search viewers as they leave, but just have it at the back of your mind that everybody is not as honest as you are. As you enter each room, simply say, "This is the billiard room", or "This is the butler's pantry", then wait for a reaction. It's a waste of time, not to say fatuous, to say things like "That's a stone fireplace". When you've shown them round, invite their questions and give answers as honestly as you can. If you don't know the answer, say so. Don't start offering cups of tea or a swift look at your holiday snaps. Such pleasantries won't sell your house. Show the viewers round and show them out.

Owner occupiers are inordinately proud of their houses and when they are conducting prospective purchasers round it shows, so the sensitive viewer will often say anything to avoid giving offence when trying to bring the visit to a comfortable close. Team viewers, such as husband and wife, will naturally wish to discuss together the merits of the house, not in front of the vendor, but after leaving, and the *real* purchaser can quite easily turn out to be the one who walks round without saying a word and succeeds in leaving you with the feeling that you have been wasting your time. So the safest plan is to ignore what a viewer says initially about his intentions and prefer to wait for further, more positive action to develop. Time and again through the book we will return to this theme of the waiting element in house buying and selling and the inordinate amount of time you have (two, three, four months) to swot up on and deal with the few things that as a D.I.Y. estate agent and conveyancer you need to know about and do.

3. Estate Agents

If you know of a really good estate agent, it will pay you to employ him, but unfortunately there are very few who will look after you in the manner described in this chapter. So if you can't find such a one you might as well do the job yourself. Though most of the remarks in this chapter are addressed to the vendors, that does not mean to say there is nothing here for purchasers, because basically all the services a vendor expects from an estate agent revolve around making a prospective buyer of his house into a real and able buyer. So a purchaser reading this, while realising that it is the vendor who pays the agent's commission, and should therefore call the tune, will also realise what he should expect of an agent, in addition to a sweet smile and a polished, up-stage manner. What's more, according to Building Society statistics, buyers become sellers, on average every seven years, and should therefore be sorting the wheat from the chaff when they are buying.

Estate Agents can be roughly divided into two categories, (i) the qualified, who carry initials after their names such as F.R.I.C.S. and A.R.I.C.S. and F.S.V.A. and have passed a number of examinations set by their societies, and (ii) the commercial, who may carry no letters at all. This does not mean to say they are unqualified, they may be extremely well qualified by practice and experience. Where letters after their names may be important, is in the answer to the would-be purchaser's question "Dare I trust this man with my deposit?" If he carries the letters F.R.I.C.S. or A.R.I.C.S. he is a member of the Institute of Chartered Surveyors who operate a joint indemnity scheme with the Incorporated Society of Valuers and Auctioneers (those with F.S.V.A.) with the aim of protecting people against the loss of their deposit when buying, leasing or otherwise acquiring property.

This scheme applies to one of their members or to a firm with at least one principal who is a member. If you need to make a claim, write for a claim form to: The Institute of Chartered Surveyors, 12 Great George Street, London SW1P 3AE, or the Incorporated Society of Valuers and Auctioneers at 3 Cadogan Gate, London SW1X 0AS. If the man to whom you so trustingly parted with your money carries the letters F.N.A.E.A., M.N.A.E.A., or A.N.A.E.A., then The National Association of Estate Agents runs a similar compensation scheme. If need be, write to them at 21 Jury Street, Warwick, Warwickshire.

If the man who asks you for a deposit is not recognisable by the heavy lettering given above, ask him if he is covered by any such scheme, and if necessary ask him to name the scheme on his receipt. If it is only an initial £10 then you can take a risk. If it is a substantial sum, you can check with your local Citizens Advice Bureau as to whether such a scheme exists. Even if the agent is not covered by a scheme, it does not mean he is a rogue. He may not have been in the business long enough to qualify, or the local agents may be of a type he does not wish to associate with. However, if you really do not feel safe in handing over your hard earned money to him, (as a stakeholder pending completion) then ask him if he has any objection (providing the person you are buying from agrees) to your asking a local bank manager to act as stakeholder. Alternatively, (if your vendor has not had the benefit of reading this book) ask if you may pay the money to the vendor's solicitor (as stakeholder). Bear in mind that the estate agent wants to get hold of the money for two reasons, firstly to help cement the sale, and secondly he then has something towards his commission.

There is the commission burglar who will promise anything when persuading you into signing an agreement that will tie you to him hand and foot for three months. Once you have put your name on the dotted line it matters not who finds a buyer who is ready, willing and able to buy, whether it be yourself or another agent — you have him to pay. His crucial ploy in getting you signed up is his assurance that he will get you a fancy price (sometimes already set by you, sometimes by him). He cynically calculates that you will become desperate to sell within two months, which leaves him a comfortable month of his agency to run during which he or someone else will come up with a buyer, often at a lower price than you could have got for yourself in the first place if you had followed the instructions herein when the house was fresh on the market.

Letters after Estate Agents' names can be important when it comes to deposits — I have shown you how to deal with that — but letters will tell you nothing about the two important things you, the vendor, need to know about an Estate Agent: (i) Can he sell the property? and (ii) can he get the best price? It is often thought that the agent who can fill a whole page of a local paper with properties for sale must be the biggest and best — wrong! The properties he is advertising are the ones he hasn't sold, and he is often waiting for them to virtually sell themselves. The best agent is often the one with few properties for sale — because he has sold up. He will get you the best price if he doesn't drag you on and on until you are desperate and will take any offer. So you want an agent who will get on with it.

Ask yourself "Could anybody ever persuade me to buy

a house which I didn't really want?" The mechanics of house purchase are so time-consuming that there is virtually no impulse-buying. Talk about "cooling-off periods", ages can go by between the viewing of a house and the signing of a contract. The exception is at an auction, where the purchaser is irrevocably bound as soon as the hammer falls, and that being so, he will have satisfied himself previously regarding the soundness of his prospective purchase. He will have his mortgage offer in his pocket before he steps into the auction room.

So when deciding on an estate agent, you should not look for a "super salesman" who can persuade people to say they will buy houses they don't want at prices they can't afford. If you do, you are obviously wasting your time. Interestingly enough, the qualities of a really good agent lie in what the law holds must happen before he is entitled to his commission; he must produce a buyer who is ready, willing and able to buy. It is often easy to find someone who is ready and willing to buy. I am sure the reader is perfectly ready and willing to buy many of the attractive dream houses he sees on his weekend trips round the countryside. Ah, but is he able? Can he raise the wind?

A good agent can produce the viewers. He does this by giving the vendor an honest opinion of what the house will fetch. A bad agent will ask the vendor what he wants for the house, and thinks to himself "that's a couple of thousand too much, but I'll take it on, and the vendor will come to his muttons later." Much better if he says "Well, Mr. and Mrs. Hope, I think you are asking a bit over the odds there. I know you have seen similar properties advertised at that kind of money, but I can tell you there's a vast difference between asking and getting. It's us chaps who see the final outcome and really know exactly how much money has changed hands".

Vendors are hardly likely to tell the general public how much they had to knock off their asking price, because it sounds like a defeat. Neither is the purchaser likely to split, because a high asking price makes him look rich, and gives him the feeling that he is living in a house worth that fancy asking price, and not what he actually paid.

A good agent will not want to lose the chance of getting the job of selling your house, no matter how daft you are, because, remember, he is short of property. At the risk of offending you, he will press on with trying to persuade you to put your property on the market at a realistic figure. Usually, you will compromise, and he will then agree to do his best at that figure for a week or two, on the understanding that you will drop the price later. If he is confident that he knows his stuff he will write into the instructions you give him, the top and bottom prices that you will allow him to take.

Having produced the viewers, and out of them all, got someone who says "Yes, I am ready and willing", you need an agent who can decide whether he is also able. You have heard of chains collapsing. That is, when A thinks he has sold to B, who can only buy provided he can sell to C who can only buy provided he can sell to D who has a 'firm buyer' to be called E. The chain collapses when any member of it withdraws for any or no reason.

A good agent is aware of the danger. So when B says he will buy, the agent asks, "Will you pay a deposit and sign a contract now?". B will reply "I will pay a deposit subject to contract". "Oh, when do you expect to be able to sign the contract?" is the next question. "When I have got a mortgage offer for £x,000" says this splendid first-time buyer. The agent who is worth his commission will then whip out a mortgage application form, complete it, and study the replies that the splendid first-time buyer has given to the questions. This same good agent will already have decided, before he ever met the prospective buyer, which Building Society will be the best for your property, and he will also know what they think a good borrower will look like. So if your buyer is too old for a long-term mortgage, or has insufficient income, your agent will courteously but firmly direct his attention to a cheaper property, for which he *will* have sufficient deposit. An agent who jokes about saying to buyers "tell me how much you want to put down, and we'll all have a good laugh and start again", is not only levelling with you but implying that he will have a go at making a fairly good buyer into a very good buyer.

If the prospective buyer says "I'll buy, but I must sell my own house", the good agent insists on knowing the asking price, looking at the property, and then advising you whether you should wait for this buyer, or forget him, because he will never get his high asking price, which is based on: so much for the Building Society, plus so much for costs, plus so much to pay off the H.P. on the car, plus so much for a new washing machine and cooker, plus so much for mother-in-law's fare to Australia (single), and so on ad infinitum; in other words, the price he would like, rather than the price the good agent knows he is likely to get.

If you have already decided on the house you want to buy, the good agent, when you instruct him to sell your present house, will without charge have a look at your proposed purchase and advise you on the price. If you haven't already found your bargain, the good agent will have a swift look at anything you have viewed and fancy, and advise you on price. If you haven't been able to fix a mortgage, he can help. Indeed he will say whether you are expecting too much from any Building Society and had therefore better forget that particular deal, even if he thereby risks losing the opportunity of putting your present home up for sale. Such an agent is a man of whom to make a business friend for life. He is treating your housing transaction as though it were his own. That is how a good agent should act for you.

When you telephone a good agent's office your calls are answered by a mature-sounding person, who, to a prospective purchaser, will appear to have bought and sold more houses than the 'receptionist' straight from school has had hot dinners. There is a place in an estate agent's office for young people to start their careers, but it isn't that of making the vital first impression on a prospective buyer. You don't pay hundreds of pounds in commission and trust your most valued possession to the tender mercies of inexperienced people. If the firm advertise that their partners are chartered surveyors and expect

you to put your faith and trust in them on that basis, then
you have a right to have your work, from start to finish, done
by chartered surveyors, and not by a person whose only qual-
ifications are in shorthand and typing. Although it has to
be said, the only thing many chartered surveyors were ever
any good at, was passing the Institute's examinations.

The instructions asked for vary. The strongest instruction
is on the basis of sole selling rights, which means, quite simply
that whoever sells, and whenever the house is sold, the vendor
will pay the agent his commission. His justification for this
is that given the assurance of his commission, he can let the
whole wide world and his wife know that your house is for
sale.

The next strongest, from the agents' point of view, is a
sole agency. This will be for a specified period, say three
months, and it means what it says, — that during the period
of the agency you will employ no other agent and if you do
he should conduct his business through the *sole* agent. However, it also means that you have retained your rights as a
principal and can therefore sell the house yourself and not
have to pay the agent a commission, although it might be a
courteous gesture to pay his out-of-pocket expenses.

Then comes the woolly sort of contract that goes something like this: We will only expect you to pay us a commission
if we sell, and we make no advertising charge. Now instructions
given to estate agents are contracts, and contracts must be
kept, otherwise all civilised business comes to an end. A contract* is a bargain or agreement and need not be in writing,
but if you intend to be able to sue on it, the problem of proving
its existence is extremely difficult, unless there is some further
evidence than your unsupported word. If when the agent
leaves your house, you haven't been asked to sign anything,
don't think you have got away with an unsupported verbal
contract because he knows all about unsupported verbal
contracts. What he does is, he goes back to his office and
has his typist send off a letter which thanks you for your
instructions, promises you his best attention, and incorporates
in the letter all the "small print" of the deal. If when you

---

*n.b.: Contracts for sale and purchase of land with buildings or without must *always* be in
writing.

receive such a letter there are points which are so woolly that you don't know what they mean, or with which you disagree, you must write back as soon as possible saying so (and keeping a copy of your letter). If you don't, a judge could take your silence as implying your consent. All that manoeuvring by an agent strikes me as pussy-footing and could indicate a similar timidness when faced by a prospective purchaser. The agent who is secure in the well-founded knowledge of his expertise will have a form which is short, to the point, and printed in readable type. He will explain it, ask you to sign it, leave you a copy of it for your bed-time reading, and assure you that if you change your mind within, say, forty-eight hours, then provided no offence is given, no offence will be taken and certainly no charge made.

Some vendors think it a good idea to let as many agents as possible have a go at selling and then pay the commission to the one who sells — a kind of winner-takes-all game, notwithstanding the elementary fact that nothing cheapens the house more than even two boards in the garden, let alone a forest. The only positive reason for engaging more than one agent is where you know of two agents who cover different areas from whence enquiries for your particular property might come — for example, in a commuter area it might be a good idea to appoint both a local agent and an agent in the area the breadwinners travel to and from earning their mortgage repayments. If your house is in an area where this consideration applies by all means get two agents on the job, but make sure that you will only have one commission to pay and that each agent will be entitled to half of it irrespective of which one of them sells.

Otherwise stick to one agent and give him a clear field, because if you get yourself into the "winner takes all" situation what do you honestly expect of any one of those agents, if he knows from the start that his hope of earning a commission is only one in two, three or even four? He is unlikely to devote his full attention to the matter and will obviously give more care and concentration to selling those houses he knows he will get a full commission for when sold.

Estate agents write the most appallingly ambiguous rubbish when advertising the charming, deceptively spacious family property, in which, in real life, you can't swing a cat round. They do the same when advertising briefly about their charges. "No sale — no charge" sounds good enough but it might mean that all you get is a mention of your house to anyone who enquires for a property such as yours. "Free advertising" might mean "we put a few lines about it in our monthly bulletin which is given out to callers and distributed to solicitors' waiting rooms where it takes its chance among a tatty pile of magazines". The only sure way is to ask. Get things clear at the beginning.

So now you know what a good agent looks like and what he should be prepared to do for you. Some agents seem either to be large shareholders in newspapers and determined to make sure there is a profit this year, or determined to be famous as a result of the acres of newsprint they cover at their clients' expense. If all the agents in your area are of the type who will put advertisements in the paper at your expense, and when a potential buyer comes along, will merely say to him, "Oh, very nice, will you tell me who your solicitor is so that we can write to him" and then concludes the service by sending a bill in, you can do without any of them, because they will do nothing for you that you cannot do with very little effort for yourself. Indeed, such agents will leave undone things which you, having read this book, will do, thus ensuring for yourself a smooth sale over which you have complete knowledge and control.

If what you have read so far does not give you sufficient confidence in any estate agent or your own power to find a good buyer and to do your own bargaining, the whole process and tricks of the trade are more fully described in "Bradshaw's Guide to Marketing Your House".

4. Viewing

First of all you must find something to view. Answering estate agents' and private vendors' advertisements in the local papers is one obvious way, and touring round finding "For Sale" boards is another. But there are also the not so obvious, such as placing your own advertisements in newspapers and even shop windows in the locality you have decided is the one for you. There is also the direct approach of knocking on doors and asking "Is this the house for sale?" to which you might be lucky enough to get the answer, "No, but that one over there is." In any case such an approach can often lead to a useful conversation about the area and its qualities and problems.

When you have viewed a number of houses within a short period of time it is sometimes, at the end of the day, difficult to remember which had what — the address alone is not always sufficient to bring the memories flooding back. So try to pick on some salient feature — the more ridiculous the better, such as "the one with the surly butler", "the one with the circular pink mirrors on the bathroom walls", "the one to suit mother-in-law", etc. and make a note accordingly on the particulars if you have got some from an agent. Remember when viewing property to which you have been introduced by an agent that he gets his commission from the vendor — he owes very little, if any, duty to a purchaser. The higher the price he gets for the vendor, the more the commission, but he's got to be a bit of a dullard if the only reason he is sticking out for the extra couple of hundred pounds is because it will push his commission from £300 to £305.

Having found a house to view your first consideration is — can I make a home here? I suggest that there are two additional criteria to which you should pay attention. The first is already at the back of your mind:- is it structurally sound? The second sounds a bit daft when you haven't yet bought, but old hands who have often been moved up, down and across the country for one reason or another will testify to its import-

ance — will it be easy to sell if ever I need to move? We will
look at each in turn.

Whether you can make a home in the house you are about
to view is a highly personal question. Nevertheless there are
a few points that are common to many people. For instance if
you are getting on in years you have to consider whether
children's screams at all times of the day and night are easily
tolerated. Even if you are young, you might well find other
peoples' kids too much to bear. A new, neat and tidy development where there is just a bunch of nice newly-married
couples but very few children, is no guarantee of a quiet life
for those who want one. Noisy, late finishing house-warmings,
followed by every other conceivable sort of party, followed by
slamming of car doors can disturb the sleep just as effectively
as the screaming children the newly-weds will soon produce!

If you are buying a semi or terrace (town/mews/cottage
style) house get to know as much as you can about who will be
doing what at the other side of that joint and party wall, and
if the vendors have the television, radio or stereogram going
full blast when you call, have it switched off and listen. When
there are neighbours' drives that you look out over try to make
sure there will not be a boat or caravan blocking your view.
Vendors who insist on viewing "strictly by appointment" often
do so because they want to manipulate the situation, — for
example if they know that at one side the neighbour takes his
bagpipe band off every week-end in his caravan, while, the
young mariner at the other takes his boat and yapping dog
away at the same time, who can blame such a vendor for
insisting on a weekend viewing? And it's a certainty that any
vendor, if questioned, will only vouchsafe that the neighbours
are quiet people who keep themselves to themselves but are
of sterling worth if called upon in a crisis, and if they think
you have an inkling that a pop group next door is trying to
perfect its line-up and get it all together on Mondays, Wednes-
days and Thursdays they will laugh that off with "Oh, it's
quite lively, we quite enjoy it — keeps you young you know.
Actually we've heard that they are splitting up — pity really".

If vendors don't mention why they want to sell and

where they are moving to, ASK. If the answer doesn't have
the ring of truth — you have been warned.

If you are a non-gardener or simply can't find the time
for Britain's major hobby don't be persuaded to buy just
because the garden looks so well established, so neat and
tidy already, and only appears to need a minimum of maintenance. All gardens need constant attention if they are to look
as though they need no attention. A shower of rain just after
you have viewed, can germinate a thousand weeds.

Any objection from any member of your family should
be listened to before you finally decide. Teenagers might say
of an open plan house that there is nowhere for them to go.
Open plan houses seem to suit the very young and the very
old, but situations near rivers don't suit either. They are too
wet for non-swimmers and too damp for the arthritic.

Before you go out viewing it is a good idea to get into
your head what hectares, yards, feet and metres look like.
Told a room is 20 feet by 14 feet or 6 metres by 3 metres,
can you visualise it in your mind? Is the bath at your present
abode of such a size that you can enjoy a long lazy soak in it?
Whether it is or not, measure it and use the size as a comparison. Will your furniture fit? If it will, that's fine. If it won't
then you have to choose — furniture or house. Having made
your first visit during the week, make your second at the
week-end (or vice-versa) so as to get a different perspective
of the neighbours and neighbourhood. Park your car some
distance away and walk — you will see a lot more of the
district that way. You are making this second visit to have
a look at the structure, and the first thing you must really
persuade yourself of, is that though you are going to the
house to poke around in somebody else's private domain you
must not be embarrassed about it. The vendors knew you and
others were likely to do this from the moment they thought
about putting the house on the market and they have had
ample time and opportunity to hide any dirty linen and to
empty the cupboards of skeletons. In any case, admit it, you
don't often get a chance to root about in other peoples' places
so get on with it, and if you get a secret thrill in the process

try not to show it.

A lot can be learned while walking up the path. A gate that is falling to bits isn't a very good introduction. Is the path itself cracking and subsiding? Is the drive likely to help or hinder when you have a flat battery? Will icing cause problems in the winter? Can you see any cracks in the stucco or brickwork? If there is a lot of zig-zag cracking around the windows and doors they are signs of old or new subsidence. If the cracks have been filled in some time ago and have not re-appeared all is no doubt well. All houses subside a little after being built and it usually expresses itself in no more than cracked plaster. But if the cracks have been filled and parted again, or worse still bricks have cracked vertically there is real trouble, as there is if a wall is starting to lean or taking on the shape of a saucer. You don't need to start digging around the foundations, or paying a surveyor to do so to know that this one is not for you — unless it can be bought for the price of the land.

While still walking slowly on the garden path, have your first look at the down-pipes, roof and chimney if there is one. Have another look up from the back garden later and if it is a tall house, bring along your binoculars so that you can inspect the chimney stack and pot. A swift look at the TV aerials in the vicinity will tell you about TV reception. If there are a lot of tall fancy ones about, reception is likely to be poor.

Once again, you are looking to see if the structure is doing the thing that a house is supposed to do: shelter you from the elements. Damp is the indicator of most structural problems in a house. Water tries to get in from the top, ends, sides and beneath. As if that were not enough, we bring it in via pipes, and builders use thousands of gallons of water in the building of a house. Houses are built of such things as bricks, mortar and wood, all of which are porous, and the soil in Britain seldom dries out so the fabric of a British house is always damp to some extent. It is when that dampness passes an acceptable level that things begin to rot and owners have to start paying out.

Blocked, overflowing gutters and cracked downpipes can

be a source of water which will penetrate in sideways, as also can badly pointed chimney stacks. Driving rain can find its way in through cracks round doors and windows. Otherwise, sideways penetration of water is very rare as modern houses are almost certainly constructed with two outside walls roughly two inches apart and pinned together by metal wires or straps. The two inch gap, called a cavity, forms an insulation barrier ensuring that water can penetrate only as far as the cavity and no further. However, in the bulding process careless builders have been known to drop mortar down the cavity and allow it to accumulate on the ties. In this case the mortar build-up can form a bridge to convey water from the outer to the inner wall. If you are buying a house in the course of construction take your torch to have a look and tell the foremen if you find his brickies are laying up problems, as well as bricks, for the future. Once a house is completed and there is no internal evidence of damp from this cause you can be pretty sure there is none. If you really want to be sure, there is only one way to find out and this applies to much else — take the house down brick by brick!

In all modern, indeed in nearly all houses there will be a damp-proof course. This is needed because the ground is nearly always damp, the brickwork in the foundations will soak it up, and it will quickly spread round the house. A damp proof course is a water-tight skin of some sort. The old system was to set slates on the third or fourth brick course above the ground, and below the level of the floor joists. Slate does not bend and the slight movements of a house can, over time, fracture parts of the slate course. For many years now, builders have used mineral felt or plastic sheet both of which are flexible and can cope with anything but a really radical structural movement. What it can't cope with is the owner who piles soil up against the wall to a height above the course. Count to the third or fourth course of bricks and you will see the slate or black bituminous material protruding a little somewhere along the line. Once you have found the height follow the line right round the house to see if your vendor has been silly. If he has, pay really particular attention to the plaster, skirting board and any other woodwork on the opposite side of that patch inside the house and give general attention to the whole of the ground floor woodwork if there are wooden floors, because damp does spread. If no real damage has been done, removal of the offending material from the outside wall is imperative. This done, check to make sure that the air bricks are clear and if the damp is only slight it will soon disappear.

What can be done when the damp course is damaged or the house was built without one? You could get a builder to go round the house knocking out a brick at a time and inserting a damp course as he goes. It might work — it will certainly be expensive. There are firms who specialize in various what can loosely be described as "patent systems". You can find them in the Yellow Pages and they will usually give a free estimate. Some of these systems have a good success rate. Most firms will give some sort of long guarantee. And here it is worth making a general point about 10, 20, 30 or even life-time guarantees and it is this: it's easy for the firm to give the guarantee, but who will guarantee that the firm will still be in business if ever you need them?

So that's the base and sides dealt with, what about the roof? The most common form of construction for residential property is a pitched roof, covered either with slates or tiles. It is often difficult to gain access to roof space, but if you have any doubts about the construction it is best to cope with the difficulty now. In the case of an old house, it is reasonable to assume that any fault in the construction itself will have developed already and your external examination will have told you whether the roof is bowing or not. If it is and has been bowed or buckled for a number of years and there is no internal evidence of damp it is probably all right. However, if you decide to have a look in the roof space take a good torch with you but keep switching it off to see if any daylight is coming in because of missing, broken or drifting slates or tiles. While you are up there you can check on insulation of ceiling, tanks and pipes and if there is none or it isn't done up to modern standards you have found another bargaining point or two.

Recent decorations can be internal evidence of damp. Vendors do titivate their houses up ready for sale but they also, sometimes, do it to cover up evidence. If you suspect this has happened see if you can borrow a damp meter from your friendly D.I.Y. shop, but be careful that you are not tracing the run of a water pipe or drain and mistaking it for damp. The instructions that come with the meter will tell you about all that.

Flat roofs need special attention. If a pitched roof covered in slate or tile goes wrong the replacement of a few slates or tiles will, more often than not, solve the problem. But the only remedy for a badly damaged flat roof is often the complete replacement of the covering. The most usual coverings are lead, asphalt roofing felt and sometimes zinc and it is important that roofs be laid to a proper fall so that water does not gather in any depressions. If you can see any such pools then trouble is on its way — sooner or later.

As the covering is exposed to heat in one season and cold in another and sometimes both on the same day, and its expansion and contraction rate is not equal to the boards on which it is laid you can often see the skeleton impression of the boarding showing through the covering. Now, that boarding should run at right angles to the gutter; if it is parallel to the gutter water will gather in the depressions which will have nothing on the depression that will settle over you when you get the builder's quotation (avoid estimates — see Chapter 15, p.155) for the repairs. Felt roofs last about ten years, asphalt up to 30 years. Evidence of downward damp then, can be seen on ceilings, upstairs walls and chimney breasts. The fault can often be located and dealt with by climbing a ladder and cleaning out the gutter. Where there are stains all round the upper walls, unless you are getting a real bargain, it might be as well to try elsewhere.

When the damp course is damaged or has not been allowed to function because soil has been piled up above it or airbricks have been blocked, you will no doubt find damage to wooden floors. It is not always easy to examine floors, particularly when they are covered with lino or carpets. A vendor refusing to let you have a careful look might give grounds for suspecting his "Oh, the floors are alright, you can take my word for it." It is particularly desirable to have a thorough examination made if there are any indications of springiness, like ornaments rattling, when you walk across the floor. Joists that are rotting allow the floor to part company from the skirting board. The floor into a bay window is the favourite place for the rot to set in and by an outside door is runner up. So if there is an inch or so gap between the skirting board and the floor boards and your vendor tells you that you can have every confidence in it, ask him to jump up and down on it for a while, after all he knows the way round his cellars better than you do.

Timbers can be affected by dry rot, beetle or woodworm. Dry rot is insidious. It is a fungus and it glories in finding a bit of damp wood to set up business in. It gets down between the fibres of wood and dries the wood out. Dry rotted wood looks as if it has been dehydrated to a brown cracked appearance and crumbles to dust at a touch when in an advanced stage of development. Unfortunately the damage is well under way before there is any external manifestation of it as mentioned above. But the conditions under which it thrives can be spotted: they are damp, smelly, unventilated corners.

Wet rot gets going when the wood becomes so saturated that the fibres break apart, weakening the wood. It tends to happen at the end of timbers (hence the attention to skirting board gaps) where water can get in between fibres, but of course, it can occur elsewhere; around sink, bath and WC wastes are likely areas. Depending on how far the wet rot has gone it can be cured, often quite inexpensively by replacing the rotted timber and rectifying the fault that caused it. Take a strong torch with you into the cellar (if there is one) because the floor joists are more likely than not to be nicely exposed for your inspection. Poke around with a strong penknife — if you can slide it into the wood at right angles to the run of the grain you've found something.

The third ill that can affect timbers is beetle or woodworm. Woodworm is the caterpillar of the beetle. The flying beetle alights and injects her egg into timber and flies away until she is ready for a repeat performance. The egg developes into a worm which, feeding off the life-giving juices of the timber, transforms itself into a beetle in the image of its mother, and burrows out into the light of day leaving behind it a tunnel in the wood and a little pile of sawdust beside it. Which all goes to show that if you simply go round, no matter how meticulously, squirting things into the worm holes, you can't be sure you have got all the little beggars and that is why you need a specialist firm in to say whether the beetle is still active, and if it is to give you a quote for pressure spraying the timbers.

To find out if the worm has been active enough to cause real danger the penknife test is used. As with the wet and dry rot, badly affected timber can be replaced and your decision must be based on the amount of repair required, so if you find evidence of wood rot of any kind, call in one of the specialist firms who will give you a quotation and offer a guarantee. If the problems have been discovered early enough the cost need not be ruinous.

There are a lot of solid floors about nowadays, so if such a floor has parted from the skirting board the supporting fill has re-arranged itself and that is why settlement has taken place — it can be rectified, but make sure there is no zig--zagging on the outer wall because in that case the foundations might be rearranging themselves too.

Another point to cover is the electrical system. A sure sign of wiring that has had its day is the plug with round pins. To be safe, no doubt the whole house needs re-wiring. In older houses during your inspections of the roof space and cellar, look out for any wires that pass across the joists. If you see two element wires twisted together and festooned along you can be pretty sure some re-wiring is necessary to bring the electrical system up to modern standards of efficiency, and above all, safety. The area electricity board will be only too glad to make a visual inspection without charge and they will make a test for about £15. As rewiring a three-bedroomed house will cost over £250 it is best to be cautious. Indeed, if for any reason the supply is cut off as it no doubt will be if there is to be any gap between the time when the vendor leaves and you move in, no re-connection will be made if the whole system is not up to standard.

Decorations can cover a multitude of sins, and are, of course, like sin, a matter of personal preference. Costs of decorating can be high particularly if you have tall ceilings, with fancy cornices or moulded ceilings. The rooms might look immaculate but always take the precaution of lifting a picture off the wall to find out if pale patches will remain when the vendor has gone. Incidentally, whether you re-decorate because you dislike the colour scheme or because the place is a dirty tip, the cost will be pretty much the same, although, if the wallpaper is already peeling off it might be cheaper!

We've dealt with unwanted water getting into the house and causing damp — now we will have a look at the water that we do want in the house. If you are to get your water from a well you will need someone to tell you if the well is sufficiently deep to avoid pollution of the water by any drains that might be or become defective. A well must also be situate at a reasonable distance from any possible source of contamination. In fact, before you go any further, a few words with the local authorities would be in order — they might already know the situation and have costly plans for the owner or his successor.

Find the tap at the highest point and try the pressure. Also try the hot water pressure to the bath — you don't want to wait all day for the bath to fill. Neither do you want to spend all day pulling on the WC plunger so drop a piece of paper into the pan and see if you can send it on its way with one shot and while you are about it note if the pan or the washbasin is cracked.

We can't deal with the drainage system in detail here but if when you walk round the garden only a portion of it is squelchy or there is an ominous line of subsidence in the driveway it might be that the vendor is a bit of a stinker and is not levelling with you. However, you can square him up by getting a firm in to test the drains. If they use the water pressure system they could cause damage so get the vendor's written permission first — as a matter of fact if the firm has anything about them they will have a standard form intended to indemnify themselves, so have a word with them to make sure it isn't amended to land you in the ...

I would like to instruct vendors not to read the next paragraph but if they can't resist reading I implore them not to draw any guide lines from it to help them with their sales! (Some hope. Ed.) Central heating systems need examining. Ask to see last year's receipts for the fuel used. If it is a system such as gas ask if it has been regularly serviced. Find a radiator at the highest point in the house and as you turn the air-release screw hold a lighted match to it. If you set up a lighted gas jet it isn't because North Sea or town gas has got into the system, it is the product of some corrosion that has started. It might only need some anti-corrosion fluid putting in the system — on the other hand that might not be sufficient. In any case all the more reason to have a careful look round for leaks particularly at joints. Leaks also tend to make nasty stains on carpets.

All the above might seem like a great song and dance production number and if you employ a surveyor to make a full inspection of the property that is exactly what the vendor will tell you he or she did. Surveyors are responsible and can be held for cash damages at law if they put it down in writing that a house is sound but experience proves otherwise. For example, when you move in together with a grand piano and a host of can-can dancing friends for a house warming party and the floor is not strong enough to support the revelry, the surveyors could have to pay for new timbers for floor and wooden legs for you and your friends. So surveyors have to be very cautious otherwise they don't get their insurance renewed. The premiums are high in any case and that, and the interminable time surveyors spend looking at property to make sure *they* are safe is reflected in their bills. It is also reflected in their reports which are sometimes splattered with some masterpieces of ambiguity such as 'so far as I was able to see,' 'in my opinion', 'further investigation might reveal, but my inspection did not lead me to believe,' and 'I could not find any evidence of......at the time.' So if you find it necessary to instruct a surveyor to do a structural inspection it might be as well to see the type, style and content of reports he has composed in the past for anxious purchasers and whether he writes positively and in such a fashion that having read such an *oeuvre* you would feel assured that the property is either sound or can be made so at a cost that you can meet, and will then be a safe investment.

If you remember most of the tips given above a vendor will not notice how much you are noticing. A glance takes in that the electric socket on the skirting board has square holes and the same glance tells you that the floor is well up to the skirting board and as you walk over to the bay to admire the view your ears tell you that the presents from Blackpool and from Malaga on the sideboard are not doing a clog-dance accompanied by castanets. And while you are admiring the view you might as well test the window to see if it opens.

So if you spot something which you think might be serious what do you do? If you think it is something you might be ready to pay to have put right, call in a firm that specialises in such work and get a quotation. If your search through the local yellow pages and a call to the local Citizens' Advice Bureau is not sufficient there are some handy addresses from where you can get some more handy addresses in Appendix II of this book.

When you have looked round the house keeping your eyes and ears open and can't pinpoint anything diabolically wrong, but have been frightened out of your wits by articles and broadcasts that labour the hazards of house purchase, and so can't trust your own judgement, what do you do? Well, you can do as recommended above and go to surveyors and get quotes for a full survey. "Ah, but I am taking a mortgage and paying the building society surveyor to do a survey, won't he tell me of anything that is wrong with the house?" you say. Well, he will and he won't. His job is to tell the building society whether the land and buildings thereon (as the saying goes) is good enough security for the money they are thinking of lending you to assist you in your purchase. He has no obligation to you, so he will not stick his neck out telling you that the structure is perfectly sound, but you can be sure that he will let the building society know if the foundations or the roof are in danger of collapse, and that whereas they think they are getting a desirable residence as security there is the distinct probability that in a year's time all that would be left for them to get their money back on would be a plot of land covered in rubble. (Incidentally it does not necessarily work quite like that. When a borrower defaults (very rare) the building society does take and sell the property. In the extremely rare case where they do not raise sufficient money to cover the defaulter's indebtedness, and their own and their agents' and solicitors' costs, then the defaulting borrower can still be sued for the balance).

Sometimes you get upsetting proof that the Society's surveyor has taken more than a glance at the house. The mortgage is offered subject to an amount being *retained* until repairs, which the surveyor specifies, are carried out. Even so, it's not fool-proof — they missed the potential disaster hidden within many timber frames.

The vendor of a property less than ten years old is apt to say that it is guaranteed by the National House Building Council. Well not quite! What a builder gets for his purchaser is a "ten year *protection*" and if you want to be more precise a "ten year structural warranty".* The protection certificate which the N.H.B.C. gives is against loss of deposit in the event of the builder's bankruptcy. For the first two years of the house life the builder has to put right at his own expense any defects which arise as a result of his failure to comply with the N.H.B.C. minimum standards of workmanship and material and if the builder goes out of business then the council takes over, but they will only find 90% of the cost, and you have to find the rest. Don't think that buying a recently-built house means that you will get a repair-bill-free ten years — you won't! A house owner is not relieved of his normal maintenance responsibilities and the agreement does not cover normal wear and tear, and normal shrinkage. As for electrical

*If so, you require the balance transferring to you. Ask the vendor to provide form HB12 on completion.

moving parts and central heating boilers they are only covered
for the first year, while fences and lifts are not covered at all.
Defects costing £40 at 1970 prices are excluded altogether.

The N.H.B.C. cover saves you from the consequences of
rank bad building and that's about it. That is to say, broadly,
the cover is for such items as subsidence or settlement, and
other major structural defects due to non-compliance with standards, such as collapse or serious distortion of joists or roof
structure, chemical failure of material affecting the load-
bearing structure, and dry (but not wet) rot. To prevent what
the N.H.B.C. call frivolous claims, claimants have to pay an
investigation fee (£20-£30) which is returnable where claims
are valid or the Council thinks it was reasonable for the
purchaser to make the claim. If you are a second or subsequent
buyer you cannot claim on the N.H.B.C. for defects which
the first purchaser reported to the builder, nor defects which
were visible, on reasonable inspection, (whatever that is) at the
time of purchase.

During its brief existence, the National House Building
Council has done sterling service for the owner occupier,
particularly the original purchaser from a builder, in raising
minimum standards of building and finish. If you are thinking
of buying a newly built house, see if the builder is on the
N.H.B.C. Register. If he isn't it might be that he has been
kicked off. On the other hand he might be a splendid upright
entrepreneural character who knows what he, like his father
before him, is about and is determined not to have any "pen-
pushers" telling him what to do. Ask some of his previous
buyers. They'll soon tell you how good he is.

You will see from the necessarily brief description given
above, some of the things the N.H.B.C. is and isn't. When you
are in any deal which involves the ten-year *structural warranty*
write off to the council and get just as much information as
you can. While we are dealing with newly built houses it is as
well to ask a vendor of a second hand house whether *he* intends
moving into one. Builders' dates for completion are seldom
kept and can often be weeks or even months wide of the mark.
Also find out if you are likely to be tagging yourself into a

chain and how long it is.

You can usefully look a vendor straight in the eyes and ask him a few pertinent questions, the answers to which could determine whether you should spend further time and money on the project. For instance, is the property freehold? If it isn't, what is the ground rent and how long has the lease to run? Does the owner have to pay any maintenance charges to anyone apart from builders, decorators etc. to whom he himself has given specific orders? Is the road and main drain taken over by the council or do the frontagers have to club up every now and then to have them repaired. If you are in a business or profession can you hang out your plate and can your spouse hang out the washing or are there any restrictions? Has anyone got the right to traipse across any part of your property? Ever? If there is any evidence (extra cookers, sinks, etc.) of more than one family living in the property what guarantee is there that they will all move out, thus ensuring that you get full vacant possession on completion. In case you are thinking of making alterations ask if the vendor happens to know if there are any restrictions in the deeds on this point, and if there aren't, whether there are any restrictions imposed by the local authority — such as a preservation order. A vendor might not declare all that he knows at this point, but don't worry too much as we have other ways of making him talk as you will learn later.

If the vendor is not there because you are viewing an empty house the back of your hand will test whether the wall is damp or not. Tearing off strips of wallpaper in order to prove your point is not very clever. But if you are viewing an old house it is clever to have a piece of bent wire with you so that you can have a cursory proddle between the bottom of the skirting board and the floor boards near any outer doors, just in case a Victorian lady or her maid dropped a sovereign she knew not where, while she was gazing into the eyes of the milkman.

Think long and carefully about buying a house which will only fit your requirements if you make a number of structural alterations. Such alterations invariably cost more

than the number you first thought of. It's the etceteras and
extras that are costly. In any case, if you are buying a house
on an estate it will be a property of a certain class and
by improving it you risk bringing it out of that class and
making it difficult to sell if and when you decide to move
again.

This is the third criterion you must have in mind when
you go viewing. Put the question: is it a good investment in
so far as I will be able to realise it without too much anguish
if ever I need to? You might think that, compared with
similar properties the one you are looking at is a snip. It no
doubt has to be, to attract a viewer at all! You don't want to
be in that vendor's situation ever, so you would be wise to
avoid buying a house situated near any of the following: a
fish and chip shop, a take-away café, a hospital, a public
house, a church, a garage or repair shop, a fire station, or a
public lavatory. All the foregoing, and a few more beside,
can be anything from a nuisance to a serious disadvantage; even
if *you* happen to be deaf and have no sense of smell, others are
not so afflicted. Any Estate Agent who knows anything at all,
knows that such badly-located properties should only be put
on the market at the height of a house-selling boom when,
literally, anything will sell. Pity really, but the message to
house owners is clear. At the first whiff of any rumour about
plans for any kind of non-residential development round
about where you live, get together with your previously
independent and apathetic neighbours and protest loud and
long at any hint of intrusion by such property-price-debasers
into what has previously been such a highly respectable area;
unless, that is, you stand to make a vast profit because the
property under discussion is your very own. In such a case
the protestors are dog-in-the-manger reactionary luddites
opposed to all forms of progress which public spirited individuals (you) are slaving away trying to introduce.

There is no doubt that for those of a nervous disposition

moving house is an activity fraught with anguish-triggering mechanisms. Surveys have shown that the two most stressful times for males are moving house and changing job. Combining the two has put many a good man into hospital. So if you have no option but to move house and job co-terminously, make your family read this paragraph — indeed show it to your doctor, acupuncturist, herbalist or transcendental meditation teacher. It's no joke — it's for real! Socrates, the Greek philosopher, was no fool. He knew, and in 400 B.C. said "man worries about those things over which he has very little or no control". The message, winging its way down the centuries is clear — keep control, do the job yourself!

5. New Houses

For young people buying their first *house* a brand new one has what can only be called a strong romantic attraction. Here they will make their attempt to create a *home*. Builders know what attracts — note how they advertise *homes* for sale when what they are trying to sell is a plan, and more often than not, a half-finished house. But when the house is finished the starry-eyed home-builders move in, secure in the knowledge that no one has been born, lived, loved, divorced or died in it. The aura of the past will not seep out of the brickwork. The dead hand of the past will not push them into outdated ways of living. It will all be new! It is all brave! But as in all romances, beauty is in the eye of the beholder — desire overpowers reason and faults and blemishes are ignored. Another great attraction of a newly-built house is that it promises to be repair-free for a number of years — if anything goes wrong it is likely to be because of a fault in manufacture for which someone else is responsible, and not wear and tear which falls to the user to put right.

There is also the National House Builders' certificate the benefits and restrictions of which we have already noted. With the certificate you have the warranty against ruinous subsidence, but some would say you can do without the nightmare experience of subsidence in the first place even though some compensation might be at hand. Given the climate in England and Wales and the rarity of a long summer drought such as experienced in 1976 the NHBC guarantees given in the past three or four years could well have expired before we experience such another drying out of sub-soils, testing the foundations and starting some nasty movements in many a dream home. So the old hands will prefer to buy a house that has been built six or seven years where any subsidence has had time to show, and where the young, vigorous first buyer will have dug the garden, sandpapered the woodwork to some kind of a finish, got some curtain rails up, some paths down and coped with the drying out procedure and the traipsing in and out of chippies trying to make the doors fit and the plumbers getting the pipework right, not to mention, if it is a big estate, the waiting while there is a big enough population to justify any local shop there might be in acquiring a decent stock of goods, in addition to the shoe-cleaning material they had a good sale for while builders' vehicles were dropping mud on the roads.

From an investment point of view it is often the case that the last house to be completed on a development is the best buy. The romantic ideas and repair-free attractions of brand new houses militate against the resale of a house on an unfinished development. A vendor can have for sale a house in which he has added a number of refinements, is offering a fair list of extras and be only asking the same price as the builder is for a brand new house, yet the vendor has to search high and low for a buyer while the developer is signing buyers up all the while, and he signs them up on a take-it-or-leave-it basis. Builders and their solicitors know how to take advantage of a situation where desire overpowers reason.

The developer appoints a solicitor who acts for him in the

sale of each of the houses on the development. Except for the address or plot number, the contract and transfer (there are one or two things you need to know about contracts and transfers — all will be revealed in later chapters) is identical for all. It is almost unheard of for any purchaser's solicitor to persuade the developer's solicitor to change any detail in the contract or transfer. You never know, it might be that they don't try hard enough. DIY conveyancers, if they see any restrictive covenants (agreements about what you can and can't do with the property — more about it later) or anything else they don't like, should try to have it altered — if you don't try you will never succeed!

Builders and their agents will often try pressurising you into signing a contract when a house still has a substantial amount of work to be done on it or even when the house has not been started. In such a case you need to be very desperate, trusting or foolish to sign up unless, at the very least, the contract is made subject to the house being completed in accordance with a set of plans, a specification, your surveyor's approval or, pretty weak but it is better than nothing, an existing show house. The less of the house you can see when you sign the contract the greater the risk.

Also try to tie the developer down to some kind of completion date. Houses are built in the open air by people relying on others for supplies of material to arrive according to the hopes and dreams of a deviser of a critical path analysis which pleased its creator when he put it on paper. But *his* Creator might send flood, storm, tempest, lightning and thunderbolt to thwart his plans, and deep down the developer knows about that. So we are introduced to the almost meaningless phrases that abound in house sale and purchase transactions, and the proviso for completion will be a slight variant on the well worn "will use his best endeavours to complete the house with all due expedition".

Sometimes builders will ask for stage payments. That is to say they will require a proportion of the purchase price to be paid when say, the footings are in, followed by more money at windowsill height, more when the roof is on, and a final payment on completion. This method can be costly, particularly if you are taking a mortgage, because at each stage the building society surveyor has to have a look, and you have to pay him a fee, and as soon as the stage payment is advanced you start paying repayments on the loan even though you might not move into the house for many a month. It's a risk.

First Time Buyers

Builders have, of late, made a determined effort to attract first time buyers and singles. They advertise as though there were some terms, prices, mortgages and services special to buyers of their houses. There are not. It is all put on the price of the house. The only help for first time buyers is the government Home Loan Scheme. So tell the builder you will do your own conveyance, get your own mortgage, pay cash – so how much discount for relieving them of all that worry? You could get a pleasant surprise provided you promise not to tell your new neighbours!

Part Exchange Schemes

Somehow find out "what's the discount for cash?" It can be considerable. If you and the combined high powered salesmanship of the local estate agentry could not find a buyer for your house, neither can the builder . . . not as the price you were asking. So consider knocking your asking price down by the combined amount of the cash discount and the agent's fees and get the house sold yourself. You can then bargain and choose with anybody anywhere and from then on get your sums right about how much your new house actually cost you and how mu :h profit you made on the last one. No builder will be upset by the tactics recommended here. His advertisement drew you to the site, he has sold a house and that is what he wants . . . the sooner the quicker!

There are a lot of risks in house buying and selling but in order to get anything done one has to take some risks. The art is in drawing the line between acceptable and unacceptable risks and each person will decide for himself where that line is to be drawn when buying a new house, or for that matter in any of the transactions outlined in this book.

6. Mortgages

Most people find that a Building Society mortgage is the best method of financing their property purchase. So for the purpose of illustration we will assume that you need to take a mortgage of £18,000 from a Building Society on a £20,000 purchase. (Later we will briefly consider other methods).

We are at the stage where you have seen the house of your dreams and finally got the seller to agree to part with it for £20,000. That suits you because you can manage a £2,000 deposit and that just happens to be 10% of the purchase price. If the vendor has an estate agent, phone down to his office, ask him what happens next and remember his reply for reference should you or any of your friends need the services of an estate agent in the future. If he can assure you that your income justifies a loan of £18,000 and your spouse thinks you can manage the repayments, fill in the application form to the Building Society the agent recommends.

If the agent turns out to be a dud, go the rounds. Start

with any society with which you are a depositor. If you draw a blank, draw out your savings too and proceed to your vendor's society, and if they can't help get the vendor to ask his solicitor. If every society you approach tells you it has a queue you have nothing to lose by putting in half a dozen applications at different societies and seeing which comes up first, provided you have been assured that your survey fee will not be expended before your application reaches the top of the pile. Some people have been known to put in multiple applications, putting down any old address as the property to be purchased, even before they start viewing. Of course, upright readers, if any, will not dream of doing such a diabolical thing and those who do have no authority to quote my name more than once.

Once you have made an application, all you need is for the society's surveyor to agree with you that the house is worth £20,000. If he does, then you get the 90% loan. If he doesn't you lose your survey fee and conclude that he doesn't know what he's talking about, and you could be right. There's many a surveyor has never bought or sold a house for himself or anyone else in his life. He may have passed all the exams; he may have come out top and got a medal for it — it doesn't mean to say he knows more about the market value of that particular house in that particular district than you do. If you do lose your survey fee there is nothing much you can do about it apart from moaning (quietly) to the Building Society's manager; often the surveyor is not employed full-time by the society and the manager can choose to whom he gives future jobs.

Also beware of the Society who will take an application simply because you or your aunty is a long-term investor. They may be short of funds. It is not unknown, in such a case, for the surveyor to down-value and the result is the same as an initial refusal, except that instead of the Society being blamed for not helping their depositor, the depositor is blamed for asking for too much.

If a society's branch has been active in the area for some time, they should have similar properties already mortgaged

to them on their books. Unless you are buying something
outlandish, you can give them a factual description and say
that it is in reasonable condition; their full-time surveyor
should then be able, sight unseen, to say within a few pounds
how much you should get without you having to risk a survey
fee.

If the society's branch has not been long in the district
and they haven't yet got a full-time surveyor, the local surveyors will be wining and dining the manager in the hope
that he will push some of the lucre their way (£30-£40 a
time). So the manager can ask them for a bit of free guidance
for you. As always, remember: if you don't ask, you don't get
to know.

If you borrow more than a basic amount from a building
society they will require some other security for their money
in addition to the property. The basic amount is usually 80%.
If you are putting £2,000 down on a £20,000 purchase the
building societies are in effect saying, "If Rake doesn't pay
his subscriptions and we have to boot him out and sell the
house we don't think that after paying all our expenses there
will be more than £16,000 left and that won't satisfy the
debt, so we had better have something in addition to the
house as security".

That something else is an Insurance Guarantee. You pay
the premium. However, if you just happen to have an Insurance Policy that has a surrender value of £2,000 or thereabouts, or a gold brick, most Building Societies will accept
either as the "further security" and you thus save yourself
the Insurance Guarantee premium, which will be deducted
from your loan and for which you get nothing except the
opportunity of a higher loan.

Something else that might be deducted is a retention.
If the surveyor thinks that the house is good security for a
maximum 90% loan of £18,000 against a purchase price of
£20,000, but he has called for a specialist report on the roof/
floors/timbers/drains and the specialist has estimated that
£1,000 worth of work is required the society will, on completion, only produce a cheque for £17,000. You then get

the work done to the satisfaction of the society's surveyor (further fee?) and the society will then release the £1,000 retention. Two things that often confuse borrowers when there has been a retention, and send them hot-foot to their solicitor or the CAB when it is too late for anything but an education job:

Firstly, building societies mean what they say — the £1,000 is retained i.e. they are lending it to you, but have put it on one side until needed to pay the builder's bills, so you are due to pay the repayments on the full £18,000 from the day of completion although you have, at the time, only received £17,000.

Secondly, please note that your deposit has, in effect, been raised from £2,000 to £3,000, because you are now buying £20,000 worth of house plus £1,000 of repairs which equals £21,000 and the mortgage available is only £18,000.

There is, as usual, a way of improving the shining hour — if you have the nerve for it — wave the offer under the vendor's nose and say, "You never told me about this awful list of repairs. I think you should stand for it." When he does you must (because the society in our example only lends 90% of purchase price or valuation, whichever is the less) amend your contract by adding a clause, "The Vendor will allow the purchaser £1,000 toward the cost of repairs." The effect at completion now is that the Vendor requires £20,000 less the £1,000 allowance equals £19,000 net. You add your £2,000 deposit to the society's cheque for £17,000 and that's the Vendor paid out. When you get the builder's bill you (quickly) get the society to bring the £1,000 out of storage and that's the builder paid out — total cash outlay for you is still the number you first thought of — £2,000.*

If you are paying swingeing rates of Income Tax; if you are sure that Income Tax rates will remain high for the next 25 years; if you are certain that your personal financial circumstances will keep you paying top rates of Income Tax for the next 25 years; if you have a copper-bottomed guarantee that Chancellors of the Exchequer won't abolish or scale

*Try for the new 90% government grant if the house was built before 1919.

down the allowances on Life Insurance Policies during the next 25 years; if you are buying a highly-priced house and your mortgage needs bust the building societies' limits; and if you can answer yes to that little lot while clutching an insurance policy which you have had for some years and which has a few thousand pounds already paid into it, then ask your insurance man for details of his company's mortgage endowment scheme.

If you are buying a highly-priced house you could also approach your bank. If you do borrow from a bank you will not get tax relief on an overdraft — therefore you need the money on a loan account. If in any doubt about what tax reliefs you can expect on your mortgage repayments ask your Income Tax Inspector for a free copy of 'Tax Treatment of Interest Paid.'"*

Borrowing short and lending long used to horrify any well-dressed and well-connected banker, but lately the banks have been sticking a toe into the housing pool. It is all so recent and spasmodic that no settled policy has yet emerged, so again, the only advice is — if you don't ask you don't get to know. Remember, whether it is Building Society, Bank or Insurance Company, they are all moneylenders, and their grand-dads, if not their dads, had bicycle clips as an essential item of their business equipment.

Though an Insurance Endowment Mortgage scheme is only for a minority of house buyers, that does not mean to say that you should not look to Insurance for help. Life Insurance which limits itself to covering the outstanding amount of the mortgage is cheap, because the chance of the Insurance company having a heavy claim is in the early years of the contract when the insured person is young, healthy, and unlikely to die, bar accidents. The schemes which insurance men can dream up are weird and wonderful in their variety and promise. No man needs endurance like the man who sells insurance — he's everybody's best friend. He has to be, the size of his commission depending by and large on the amount of your premium. Many of his schemes would be a treat if young people, starting out to build a home, had not so many

* Caution: Tax relief on interest paid on mortgages might be scaled down or abolished some day.

other uses for their money. So stick to the simple point that you want cover providing that if you live you get nothing back from the Insurance Company, but if you die, then they will put enough cash into your widow's hand to pay off the outstanding mortgage.

A young man of 25 who takes a mortgage of £18,000 on a 25 year term at 15% can get himself a mortgage protection policy for as little as £27 per annum gross, and actually pays £23 net of tax, so for less than 50p per week he can make sure that his wife and children can live rent free for the rest of their lives, should he predecease them. If a young wife does not make sure of that she's a fool — if she wants more she's greedy. Any young man who has a wife he cares about and has, or intends to have children, is every kind of improvident person if having read the above, he fails to take out a Mortgage Protection Policy.

Because tax relief is given on interest paid on loans raised to buy property, it doesn't mean to say that you will always be on a winner. There are tens of thousands of people around who could pay off their mortgages, but don't, because they get tax relief on the interest paid. Unless you can invest the money to fetch in a higher net return than the net you are paying out, get it paid off. It is silly to pay £1 in interest to a building society, so that you can get 30p knocked off your tax bill!

In case you are wondering how you would cope with paying off your mortgage in order to lay your hands on the deeds for handing over on completion of a sale, this is how it is done. Get to know the exact amount of money required on the due date (called a redemption figure). At the same time ask if the lender's solicitor will give you and the purchaser's solicitor "the usual" undertaking to send the deeds on after completion in return for a banker's draft made payable to the lender which will be handed to you at completion for onward transmission.

It is sometimes thought that it is best to leave something outstanding because then the Building Society is taking care on your behalf of the deeds or the Land Certificate (you will be learning about the difference between these two soon).

There is no reason why you should not keep the deeds safely at home under the piano lid. The documents are no good to a thief. Vacant possession of the property has to go with them before they have value. If you are afraid of fire, you can deposit them (free) at your bank. If it is a Land Certficate you need not be afraid of theft or even fire if you take a note of the Registered number and keep that safe.

Certainly the last place on earth to leave deeds or Land Certificates is a solicitor's office. I have seen piles of deeds on open wooden shelves, stuffed into old sideboards and, at best, 'fire resistant' metal cupboards. A solicitor likes you to leave valuable documents with him. He can't advertise or tout for business (or so the Law Society rules say) so he tries to make sure that you will go to him again and again. So well and good if he happens to be God's gift to the fearful and benighted, but it is nice to be able to change. There is power in holding them thar deeds — so have that power for yourself. Get them into the old homestead or safely tucked under the piano lid as did the old gent, to whom I will introduce you later.

7. Contracts

A contract is an agreement to do something. It is constituted when parties accept one another's offers. Any number of people can be parties to the contract. Parties must be identifiable and over 18 years old. Lunatics and some drunkards are debarred. What transforms a simple agreement into a contract is that the contract is made upon a consideration. Consideration is a matter of inducement for something promised, so it has to be valuable, and in this day and age, for most people, what could be more valuable than money?

A vendor's contract says, in effect, "You, Mr. Rashley, have induced me to promise you vacant possession of my house by offering to pay me £20,000." And if Mr. Rashley, having put his signature to this agreement (upon a valuable consideration of £20,000) called a contract, fails to keep the bargain, then he is sueable on that contract.

On pages 53 & 55 you will find my suggestions for contracts. One is for the sale of registered property, the other for unregistered. All the main headings required for a second-hand freehold house situated in England or Wales are there. If you are selling, type three copies up as soon as you have your buyer's particulars. If you are buying, and a vendor's solicitor tries slipping in anything more than my examples at 53 & 55 show, such as "the purchaser does not rely on any statements made by the vendor", have it struck out at draft stage.

If your vendor is one of the bold kind, you will receive a draft as illustrated. If you buy from Mr. Feather, prepare to receive a draft contract from his solicitor, Mr. Skinner. The solicitor's contract will be a printed one, of the type bought in by the gross, and the typist will have filled in the few blank spaces. It is the typed-in bits you need to study.

Solicitors choose from two sets of forms, and use either "Law Societies' Conditions of Sale" or "National Conditions of Sale". Most seem to prefer the latter. Both forms are copyright. Only solicitors may buy them — they are not available to the public.* In case you have spotted that I am enticing you to refer to the National Conditions of Sale at my clause 6, n.b., I am only referring to the National Conditions, not copying them. These National Conditions are a useful summary of the general law, in so far as it applies to such contracts, and they occupy line after line of fine print in a solicitor's contract. So stand well back and if any of it has been altered, have a closer look, and if you still don't know what is going on, ask for an explanation.

Ignore the fine print, except in the unlikely event of you being involved in an auction, or a manorial transaction which has the benefit of bestowing benefices. If you are the vendor, just remember you want the money, if a purchaser you want the house. Contracts for sale of land (in our case with buildings on) usually include the following:

a) **Description of the parties,** i.e. names, addresses and occupations of both vendor and purchaser.

b) **Description of what is being sold.** A plan of the area should accompany the draft contract. If the property is unregistered there will be a plan amongst the deeds, so get a photo-copy done (see Chap. 12) If registered, you will receive a copy of the plan with the office copies. (Something else which you will learn about in a few pages time).

Included in the description of what is being sold should be a recital of any rights there might be, such as light, water, way, drainage. But as per my suggested contracts, they are usually referred to in

*OYEZ Law Stationery Society says that "If any member of the public asks for a National Conditions of Sale Contract they will not be refused." 1983.

general terms at this stage, and answered in a little more detail when the requisitions (i.e. questions) on (about the) title (ownership) are received.

c) **The price.**

d) **The amount of deposit** and how it is to be paid and by whom it will be held acting as stakeholder (agent /bank manager/solicitor or vendor and purchaser who open a joint bank account for this purpose only).

e) **The date for completion.** Usually this is fixed at one month after the exchange of contracts. The purchaser should pay the balance between the deposit paid and the purchase price on the completion date, and in exchange, the vendor should give full vacant possession. What, you may ask, happens if either side finds that they can't complete to the exact date? Well, I suppose this is one of the thousand things which could go wrong. But don't be frightened, and worse still, don't despair — it isn't a legal problem yet. Whether you are doing the job yourself or paying Mr. Skinner the hiccup would have occurred and the inconvenience would have been yours to solve.

If your opposite number to the contract gives what sounds like a good reason for delay, then you must come to some new understanding. And if your vendor is being silly and saying he wants more money, has changed his mind about the house he wanted to buy and move into, or, simply changed his mind, full stop, then you have to make some decisions. What are your options? If it is a postponement, you can simply accept his new date. But if you decide that the contract should be kept then you must give the other party written notice to complete. The notice must be reasonable and take into account the circumstances of the particular case. A month's notice seems to be usual, but if you are faced by this very unusual circumstance, have a look

at the National Conditions of Sale. If you came
across a problem with your washing machine that
turned out to be beyond your D.I.Y. expertise, you
would not be afraid to consult a dealer, so, if after
giving notice you have not got a sensible new arrangement, then consider going to a solicitor for
advice. Decide what your problem is, and then ring
round for quotes from the local legal luminaries.
The only circumstance where either or both of the
parties to the contract can insist that the contract
be completed or come to an end on the very date
given for completion is where a clause is inserted
in the contract to say that time is the essence of the
contract. If time has been made the essence and,
say, the purchaser says "but I can't complete until
the day after the date specified for completion," the
vendor is at liberty to put the contract at an end and
confiscate the deposit. If it is the vendor who cannot
complete and time was the essence, the purchaser
can demand his deposit back (note why we need
stakeholders) put an end to the contract and possibly
sue for damages.

f) **The capacity in which the vendor sells**

    i) 'Beneficial owner' is the one you will come across
most often. It means what it says and can be
used in the singular or plural.

    ii) 'Tenant for life'. This vendor is entitled to sell
the freehold or leasehold, though his interest
is only for his lifetime: nevertheless he has wide
and unfettered powers of dealing with the land
and can give a valid receipt for capital money
arising on a disposition of the land so you need
not fear him.

    iii) 'Mortgagee'. This is where the mortgagor (he
who borrowed) has defaulted, & the mortgagee

(he who lent) has taken possession. You will be well advised not to sign any contract or pay any real deposit to anyone until you see, with your own eyes, that a property being sold by a mortgagee is in fact totally empty. If you believe in belt and braces, have a swift look to see if the door locks have been changed. If they haven't ask the vendor to see to it before you make the next move.

iv) 'Personal Representative' is an executor or administrator who is disposing of the property of a deceased person, and has the rights and duties of one so appointed (see p.155) and he will have official papers to prove it and a purchaser will need to see that proof.

g) **Extras:** Items which are not fixtures and fittings, which can pass by delivery, and have been bargained for separately are sometimes included by reference to a separate inventory. If included in the purchase price (stated in the contract) and a separate value has been agreed for them, that price is stated in this clause particularly if doing so will reduce the stamp duty payable on the transfer or conveyance (more about this later).

h) **Restrictive covenants.** These are notified to the purchaser in the contract and a full copy is attached to the draft contract. The clause in the contract will say that the purchaser, having been supplied with a copy, is deemed to have full knowledge of them, and no requisitions (questions) nor objections shall be raised in respect thereof. Normally this means that the vendor will answer questions about the covenants having been kept, but that he is not getting himself involved in trying to get any of them changed. Vendors should watch out for solicitors Clever, Dick and Skinner, who will pick out a really impen-

etrable lump of verbiage in the list and will ask
you what it means. The reply is so simple — "it
means what it says." After all, it was their colleagues
Bull, Patt and Flopp who wrote the original, not you.

i) **Freehold or leasehold** — In the latter case the
lease should be referred to. Put the lease through
the copier and attach to the draft contract.
Again provide in the draft contract that there
are to be no requisitions or objections, but be
prepared to answer sensible questions if you
know the answer for sure.

j) **The rate of interest** to be paid for the period between
the completion date in the contract, and the date on
which completion actually happens. Fix the rate at
a little above your bank's minimum lending
rate, or the prevailing Building Society rate.

k) A statement about how the vendor intends to prove
he is the owner. This is done by: i) saying that office
copies and an authority for the purchaser to inspect
the register will be supplied, or ii) quoting a conveyance of the property which is at least 15 years old.
More about (i) and (ii) later.

So that's what a basic contract is all about. Further
clauses can be added, and in the crusade against the gazumper
on the one hand and the breaker of promises on the other
there follow my suggestions for some added clauses which
have already saved thousands from nervous breakdown.

CONTRACT FOR SALE
OF REGISTERED LAND

THIS CONTRACT is made the   day of   nineteen-hundred and   BETWEEN Clint Bold & Constance Bold his wife both of 14, Plevna Place, Blossomton, (herinafter called the Vendors) of the one part, and Cecil Feather and Camilla Feather his wife both of Sniff Yard, Pitchborough (herinafter called the Purchasers) of the other part.

WHEREBY IT IS AGREED the vendors will sell and the purchasers will buy: the freehold house No. 14, Plevna Place, Blossomton, Edenshire, as registered at the Land Registry with title absolute under Title Number ED999707 for the sum of £20,000 (twenty thousand pounds) SUBJECT to the following conditions:

1. A deposit of £2,000 (two thousand pounds) shall be paid to Messrs. Locke, Stock, and Barrell of 77, Bargain Lane, Blossomton Estate Agents [Fred Steel of 27, Hight Street, Blossomton, Bank Manager] on exchange of contracts and shall be held by them /him pending completion as stakeholders.

2. Vacant possession shall be given to the purchasers on completion which shall take place on   198

3. The Vendors sell as Beneficial Owners

4. The property is sold subject to the restrictive covenants and matters referred to by or set out in entries number......of the charges register and referred to or set out in the property register copies of which are to be or have been given to the purchasers' solicitors, no questions shall be asked nor objections made in respect thereof.

5. The vendor shall produce to the purchaser a good and sufficient title to the property hereby contracted for by the supply of Office Copies of the register and filed plan, and an authority to inspect the register.

6. National Conditions of Sale insofar as they are not inconsistent with these conditions shall apply to this contract and the prescribed rate of interest shall be 2% above ....bank base rate.

7. Included in the purchase price are the following items:

8. (any other "subject to......" clauses).

54

Application by Purchaser for Official Search with priority in respect of the WHOLE of the land in a title

..........*local*.... District Land Registry

Send to address from
Appendix 1
no fee required

(For an official search of part of the land in a title. use form 94B).

County and district (or London borough)	*See appendix 1*
Title number	*Vendor gets from Land Certificate (P87 P64)*
Enter full name(s) of the registered proprietor(s)	*Vendor's*
Application is made to ascertain whether any adverse entry has been made in the register since the date shown opposite being EITHER the date on which an office copy of the subsisting entries in the register was issued OR the last date on which the land or charge certificate was officially examined with the register.	*See P.75*
Enter full name(s) of the applicant(s) *(i.e. purchaser(s) lessee(s) or chargee(s))*	*Yourself*

I/We ~~as solicitors acting for~~ the above mentioned applicant(s) certify that the applicant(s) intend(s) to:-

(Enter X in the appropriate box opposite)

X	P	purchase
	L	take a lease of
	C	lend money on the security of a registered charge on

} the WHOLE of *
the land
in the above
title

* *if newly-built use*
Form 94B

A WHERE A SOLICITOR IS ACTING FOR THE APPLICANT(S)

I/We certify that I/We hold the duly signed written authority of (or of the solicitor(s) for) the above mentioned registered proprietor(s) to inspect the register of the above title OR that I/We also act as solicitor(s) for the registered proprietor(s).

Indicate this by entering X in this box

| | A |

B WHERE A SOLICITOR IS NOT ACTING FOR THE APPLICANT(S)

The duly signed written authority of (or of the solicitor(s) for) the registered proprietor(s) to inspect the register of the above title accompanies this application.

Indicate this by entering X in this box

| X | B |

* *See P.64*

Key number	Signed: .... C. Bold
	Date: ....
P. BOLD	Telephone number
14, PLEVNA PLACE	Reference: *(use your initials and the date)*
BLOSSOMTON	

This panel must be completed using BLOCK LETTERS and inserting the name and address to which the official certificate of result of search is to be sent.

CONTRACT FOR SALE
OF UNREGISTERED LAND

THIS CONTRACT is made the   day of   198
BETWEEN Clint Bold and Constance Bold his wife both of 14, Plevna
Place, Blossomton (hereinafter called the Vendors) of the one part,
and Cecil Feather and Camilla Feather his wife both of Sniff Yard,
Pitchborough (herinafter called the Purchasers) of the other part.

WHEREBY IT IS AGREED the Vendors will sell and the purchasers
will buy: the freehold dwelling house known as 14, Plevna Place,
Blossomton, Edenshire, as the same was conveyed by a conveyance
to the Vendor dated fifteenth day of October 1957, FOR THE SUM
of £20,000 (twenty thousand pounds) and SUBJECT to the following
conditions:

1.   A deposit of £2,000 (two thousand pounds) shall be paid to Messrs.
     Swift & Sure of 77, Bargain Lane, Blossomton Estate Agents/
     Fred Steel of 27, Hight Street, Blossomton Bank manager on
     exchange of contracts and shall be held by them/him pending
     completion as stakeholder.

2.   Vacant possession shall be given to the purchasers on completion
     which shall take place on   198

3.   The Vendors sell as beneficial owners

4.   The property is sold subject to the restrictive covenants and
     matters referred to by or set out in the above mentioned con-
     veyance to the Vendor, copies of which having been given to the
     purchasers' solicitor, no objections shall be made or questions
     asked in respect thereof.

5.   The vendor shall deduce to the purchaser a good and sufficient
     title to the property hereby contracted for, the root of which
     shall be a conveyance between A and B dated......

6.   National conditions of sale insofar as they are not inconsistent
     with these conditions shall apply to this contract and the pres-
     cribed rate of interest shall be 2% above the........bank base rate.

7.   Included in the purchase price are the following items:

8.   (any other "subject to......" clauses).

8. Gazumping

The state of high tension into which many vendors and purchasers get themselves is caused by the uncertainty during what seems to be the interminable time which elapses between a buyer and a seller saying I do and the promise being committed to paper. What causes the delay? The usual reasons are two. Firstly the purchaser needs to sell his present abode to raise the money for his purchase, or vice-versa, the vendor has to find suitable alternative accommodation; and secondly the purchaser needs to make sure of his mortgage for his purchase.

A contract, as we have seen, needs a completion date. Say everyone would like to complete in August but the vendor isn't sure that he will be able to find himself a bargain to move into by then, or the purchaser isn't sure that the building society will lend him the amount he requires, or the purchaser is not sure that the man he is trying to sell his house to will sign on the dotted line, then what is simpler, if there is goodwill on both sides, than to enter clauses which provide for these things to happen before the contract becomes binding? If all concerned would like, at best a completion date in August, enter a completion date of September or October and add the magic words "or before". So for those hoping to complete on August 20th the clause would read "Completion will take place on or before 20th October". It is like being in a small boat and throwing out an anchor as far as you can onto the land. You know the boat is secure and that you can proceed to pull the boat towards firm land when your meal is ready ashore.

If the main stumbling block is the mortgage an extra clause can be inserted saying "subject to an offer of a mortgage of £x for a term of x years being received from the Openhand Perpetual Building Society on or before [date]". You might think it necessary to specify the building society and term of years as above in case some smart alec dragged you round from one building society to another with a survey fee to be paid to each.

How about the man who is relying on the sale of his own house to finance his purchase? He should have had his own house on the market before he met up with his prospective vendor and so have one or two irons in the fire. Certainly he should know, by now, whether his asking price is within the bounds of reason. So to put his vendor's mind at rest he can, with confidence, sign a contract which contains a clause: "Subject to a binding contract for the sale of 10 Sniff Yard at the price of at least £x being received by the purchaser on or before......" and here enter at least one month before the completion date on the contract because when *his* own purchaser signs up he will usually require the completion to take place one month after the signing of his contract.

A couple of possible objections from a purchaser could be: is it safe to sign up before the searches are done, after all, there might be plans for a road to run right through the house; and what about title — how do we know the vendor really does own the house? The latter point is already taken care of at clause 5 in both of our contracts (a standard clause in all property contracts) and if the vendor cannot come up with the goods to fulfill that clause then the contract falls. As for the searches — if you are taking a mortgage there is no hope of a building society lending if the searches don't come good, so your "subject to mortgage" clause covers you. If you are buying for cash a swift trip to the local council offices with a form listing all the questions you need answering before you sign up is necessary (see p. 96).

If you are not employing an estate agent in your sale, who as part of his service to you should advise on the purchaser's chance of raising the minimum figure specified, ring round and get quotes from the local agents for doing the job of going for a quick look at the property, then ringing you back (no written report required) to let you know how much the purchaser's house should fetch.

If any of the above subject clauses are added to a standard form of contract such as is produced on pages 53 & 55 it is a conditional contract. Nothing new in that. As explained earlier the standard forms solicitors use contain a plethora of conditions, indeed their titles tell you so — "National *Conditions* of Sale" and "Law Society's *Conditions* of Sale". Look at our own specimen contract. Doesn't it state SUBJECT to the following *conditions*, which turn out to be seven in number with space left for more to be added. So what you have is a conditional contract and it is incumbent on the parties to it to to make what is contracted for come about *within the limit of those conditions.*

Now you might say "If a vendor accepts a conditional contract such as is suggested here, isn't he giving the purchaser a free option?" Not quite, go back to the chapter on Estate Agents and re-read how one doesn't take some looney seriously who is trying to get £20,000 for a house worth £15,000 at most or some discharged prisoner who *hopes* to get a £12,000 mortgage on the strength of a job he *hopes* to get a week next Pancake Friday. With an option the prospective purchaser can simply let the option run out and forget his option monies if he finds a better house at a cheaper price or change his mind for any other or even no reason, but with a conditional contract the purchaser can only bring it to an end if the conditions turn out to be unfulfillable in the specified time, (or, indeed, when the contract is completed to the satisfaction of all).

Another question the astute reader might well ask is, "If it is all so simple to tie up, why don't solicitors and estate agents already follow this method thus saving their clients a great deal of anxiety?" The reason I offer, and it is founded on wide experience, participation and observation, is that most sales go through anyway. If a vendor loses his purchaser — in the fullness of time he finds another. If a purchaser misses the house of his dreams — well he hadn't realised that there are more fish in the sea than ever came out of it — he soon finds an alternative. The professionals concerned do not mind how much sleep is lost in the process, provided it is not their own.

Having become accustomed to taking selling and conveyancing in their stride and knowing that things nearly always get cobbled together one way or another, the professionals tend to think of their uninitiated clients as at best a brood of worriers and at worst a bunch of neurotics. So the best they can say to the concerned client is "there, there, you will just have to be patient" and when the whole deal collapses "I'm sorry but these things happen, as you know there is many a slip twixt cup and lip". If your parsnips are easily buttered, that's O.K. but for those who, once they put a hand to the plough, like to get the job done, it is almost insupportable, and another good reason for doing your own conveyance, or even if you don't, using these pages as a check list on what good solicitors and estate agents should be doing for their money.

As a vendor you should allow as few subject clauses as possible, and those you do allow need to be virtually certain of fulfillment to merit inclusion in the contract.

As a purchaser do not hesitate to ask for the subject clauses. Do not be afraid of the vendor because you know from your own experiences of trying to sell a house or even a car, the high state of anxiety one can work oneself into. The vendor's friends at the pub and at work might say that he will be a mug to let his house go so cheap and he ought to hang on for the extra £1,000, but he knows deep down what a bird in the hand is worth particularly when there is a mind bending cacophony of sound coming from the bush. He will consider it cheap at the price to rid himself of the tension particularly when he can rationalize it by saying "Well, I was never the greedy type, and anyway, it's worth it to put the wife's mind at rest".

You can put more or less anything you like into a contract
providing your opposite number will agree to it. If you come
across a vendor who steadfastly refuses to sign a contract with
the kind of conditions suggested here it is because, no matter
what he says, he is hoping to be a gazumper — so beware.
If you are determined to have his house and eventually get
yourself into a position where you can sign an unconditional
contract, having got your mortgage, and got your own house
sold etc., quite a few weeks will have passed and your vendor
will have exposed to you the fact that there was not a queue
of excited people wanting to buy — so give him the medicine
— reduce your offer.

If you have a purchaser who will not sign up as suggested
it is because he is hoping to see something cheaper and/or
better in the intervening weeks or he will only move house if he
can get an astronomical price, or he is just weak-kneed. So
keep your house firmly on the market and no matter how
sorry you feel for such a supplicant give no promises except
those which are reciprocated on paper.

9. The Registers

There are two systems of land conveyancing in England and Wales: the registered system in which case title to the land is registered at the Land Registry, and the unregistered system where the title is not registered at all. The unregistered is the older, but not many years will pass before all land is registered and thus conveyancing property made much simpler for all. By the way, all references to land include everything built on it.*

Official records of the property with which you are about to deal may be found in three places:

1. **The Local Council** who are entitled to keep a register of notices affecting dangerous structures, public notices about infringements of building regulations, compulsory purchase orders, smoke control zones and other things the local authority want to make sure do or do not happen to the property. When we come to it you will see that you quite easily find out about that little lot by the simple expedient of sending off a couple of forms (LLC1 and CON29) which have printed on them all the questions you need to ask.

2. **The Legal Charges Department** at Plymouth which keeps a register of various charges (mortgages), interests and notices such *as* second mortgages and Class F charges (right of spouse to occupy the matrimonial home) which cannot be

*It helps if the DIY Conveyancer gets an early grasp of the fundamental point that **all** conveyances are of LAND, whether built on or not. Whether it sells for a million or one pound and one pence, the recipe is the same.

registered at the Land Register because the Land is not registered. Pending writs or order (bankruptcy) and pending action (bankruptcy) are also kept at Plymouth, and you will need to send off a form K16 to find out about any bankruptcy orders, writs etc. whether you are buying on registered land or not.

3. **The Land Registry** is the third place where official records of land transactions are kept. This is the one that did the trick of simplifying the act of transferring the ownership of a house from one owner to another. Where a house is on registered land all the tiresome business of proving title, and tracing back the covenants and conditions through a series of conveyances is dispensed with because it was done once and for all when the title was registered. And not only that — when the Land Registry sends you a copy of the register which shows that Feather owns the property a state guarantee is incorporated in it. When you have a Land Certificate produced by the Land Registry showing you as the owner, that ownership is guaranteed by the state.

Initially the Land Registry Act covered only London and made registration of title compulsory for any sale which took place after 1898 in that area. No extension of the compulsory system of registration was made until 1925. From 1925 the system of registration has been gradually extended to further areas and will eventually cover the whole country. So, if you buy a house in Banbury, Oxon. (unless it is on a biggish, newish development) in 1980 you will not have to register it, but you will if you buy in Bolsover, Derbyshire. If your vendor in Bolsover bought before March 1977 he did not have to register, because compulsory registration for that area had not come in by then.

Strictly speaking it is the title of the owner of land that is registered and not the land itself, but for simplicity's sake we will refer to the land whose owner's name is registered, as registered land. The piecemeal extension of the registration system means that if you are buying in Lambeth you can be certain that the title will be registered unless it has been in the same ownership since February 1900 (or before); on the other hand, not many properties in South Derbyshire will be registered because registration only became compulsory in 1978.

Until 1966 any owner could voluntarily apply to have his ownership registered. But in 1966 registration became limited to compulsory areas plus those cases where the registrar can make an exception e.g. where the title deeds were lost or destroyed during the war, or where there are complex building developments taking place.

If you went to the Land Registry and looked at the actual register, what is produced on pages 71 & 73 is what you would see. It is also what would be reproduced on the Land Certificate in Mr. and Mrs. Smart's possession if they had no mortgage. In view of Charge No. 5 in the Charges Register the Land Certificate will be held at the Land Registry and a Charge Certificate will have been issued and held by the Building Society as proof of their interest.

If you ever lend any money, don't feel as secure as can be, just because the borrower hands over the Land Certificate. He could sell the property purporting to have lost the certificate and you would have lost your security. A mortgage on registered land does not hold unless the Land Certificate is in possession of the Land Registry and a charge certificate has been issued to a mortgagee (he who lent). A charge certificate only differs significantly from a land certificate insofar as it has a different cover, and of course the Charges Register shows the mortgage in the former.

Though we refer to the Land Registry (singular) it contains a number of registers (plural). These are:- The Property Register, Proprietorship Register and Charges Register. The references made to your property in these registers constitutes what used to be known as the deeds to your property and can consist of as few as four pieces of paper having as little as two dozen lines of typing on them.

The Registrar will supply copies ("office copies") of these entries to any registered proprietor. You are still the registered proprietor even though you only appear to own a tenth of the property, and the Building Society the other nine tenths. The registers at the Land Registry are confidential and only the registered proprietor, her or his solicitor or persons authorised by the proprietor may inspect and obtain copies of the entries. The Land Registry do not have an official form for this purpose, so if you are a vendor give — if a purchaser expect something like this:-

> We Clint Smart and Constance Smart the registered proprietors of 14, Plevna Place Title No. EDN999707 hereby authorise Thomas Bold and Prudence Bold of ....
> to inspect the register of Title No. EDN 999707 and any filed documents referred to therein.
> Sign   date

The key to unlocking the files at the Land Registry is the Title number, i.e. a reference number. Every registered house has one. The title number appears at the top of each page of the office copies which will be supplied to you. If you aren't certain whether or not the property is registered, obviously you will not have the number and will send off a Form 96; the Registrar will return it and if the house is registered he will give you the title number. If you are an intending purchaser you will need to attach the owner's authorisation to your Form A44 (more about all these forms when we come to your actual use of them). If you do know that the house is registered but don't know the Title Number, write in the box "please supply number", and hey presto the obliging staff (and they are) at the Registry will supply it.

So that you can see how the Land Registration system works in practice and what a pleasant surprise awaits you when the simplicity of it all is proved to you, on the arrival of the office copies let us take a look at a set (reproduced by kind permission of the Controller of Her Majesty's Stationery Office) which shows the various types of entry which could appear on Mr. and Mrs. Smart's title to No. 14 Plevna Place, Blossomton, Edenshire. Title Number 999707. Office Copies are photo copies of everything which is entered on the registers at the Land Registry concerning the land (property) with the title number quoted. See pages 71 and 73.

A swift look through our example will convince you that it is mostly self-explanatory; where it is not immediately clear, hold tight, just a little detective work and clarity is at hand. However, first of all note the number of pages and check you've got them all. Just for fun the register of your property may consist of say five pages and you only get three. Don't panic, it turns out that two are blank, and somewhere on your office copy it will be noted "pages 4 and 5 are blank. Not photographed".

Section A: Property Register simply describes the land. Usually the postal address is all that is shown because that is sufficient to identify it. Sometimes as in our example there is also a plan attached. In this section there is also mention of Entry 2 in the Charges Register — its bark is worse than its bite — more about it later.

Section B: Proprietorship Register. Here we see that in our example the proprietor has Title Absolute, and this is the one that you will usually come across. It is the best class of title and applies to ninety-nine per cent of freeholds. The Registrar only gives the description Title Absolute where he is entirely satisfied about the owner's ownership of the property. Title Absolute means that the ownership is guaranteed by the state.

A leasehold property might have title absolute. This is only so in cases where the Registrar can guarantee that the lease was validly granted, i.e., the lessor (granter of lease) actually owned the land. Good leasehold title is shown in those cases where the superior title has not been investigated by the Registrar. Solicitors seem to treat both as equally valid.

Possessory Title: This is very rare indeed. It is the weakest form of title and if, as a purchaser, you come across it, go to the reference library, (book titles will be given later) and after reading up, discuss with your vendor what is to be done, and then decide whether to go forward with the purchase. But n.b. a possessory title is a kind of squatter's title which gets stronger the longer it exists.

The Proprietorship Register shows the present owners. The names of previous owners are struck out. In the remarks

column the price paid is often shown. Sometimes the price
is not shown so we have given both. If you are forwarding
office copies to a prospective purchaser and you don't want
him to know what you paid, black it out. Each sheet of the
office copies will carry the legend printed at the foot of the
example: "the subsisting entries on the register on (in this
case) 3rd October, 1978", and it is of importance as you will
see later, so keep your eye on it.

Section C: Charges Register. This is where the elementary
detective work comes in. So gather round while I tell you the
story behind the sample produced here.

On 16th March, 1967 a teetotal farmer called Thomas
Dick sold his smallholding together with his house and rhubarb
shed to Charles Harry on condition that Mr. C. Harry wouldn't
do any further building and wouldn't convert the house to a
pub or the shed to a disco. The years went by and Mr. C.
Harry got it into his head that he would like to build
a few houses on the land, so on his accountant's advice he and
his Mrs. formed Sunshine Investments and tried to look up
Mr. T. Dick, but he couldn't even be dug up, for he had
been cremated. They therefore searched out his kith and kin,
and found, as is sadly the case in such matters that kith & kin
reacting against the strong strictures of husband and father,
had turned to the bottle with a vengeance, once he was out of
the way, and now being on the hard times he had failed to
convince them would befall if they took the downhill path,
were easily persuaded to remove the restriction on building
— for a consideration. Sunshine Investments alias Mr. C.
Harry built the houses and sold one to Mr. Feather, who subsequently sold to Mr. Smart, from whom you now wish to
purchase. However, before Sunshine Investments were able
to do their bit towards solving Mr. Feather's housing problem
(their own too) the Blossomton Council planning committee
had to be pacified, and they made it a condition that no-one
actually went to live in the new houses until the new main
sewer being built from Here to There had been completed.
(As the condition has obviously been complied with, the entry
is now of no interest to anyone).

Sunshine Investments also got themselves a solicitor, Mr. Newman. He was a young solicitor, and being rather inexperienced in the business thought that creating the legal framework was all art and no science. Like all young artists he didn't know when to stop. He got out the volumes of Forms and Precedents, got every reference on restrictions, covenants, exceptions and reservations, and tacked them on to every transfer to every purchaser. It mattered not that there were no cess pits, he put in the rules governing cess pits, and preceeded the rule with the words: "if ever there be......"

The Registrar couldn't put all Mr. Newman's blatherings onto the Charge Certificate, but they existed, so he puts "copy in certificate" in the remarks column, and sends you a copy. Sometimes the copy will consist of the last conveyance which was drawn before the Land became registered. In any case it will list the restrictions on the property. And that is the copy that the vendor must attach to the draft contract as mentioned at our clause 4 in "Contracts". This is what you are buying.

As pointed out earlier, there is nothing you can do about restrictive covenants. You either accept them or buy elsewhere. Anyway, have a look through them, and if you had intended putting up kennels for dog-breeding purposes and find that there is a restriction on using the land for any business purpose, put your thinking cap on. If there is no other property around you'll be pretty safe, but if the house is on an estate no doubt all the other houses have similar restrictions entered on their titles. You would only need, as a neighbour, one light sleeper who never seemed able to go shopping without stepping into a pile of ordure, for your life to be made a misery and your doormat littered with summonses. That said, there is unlikely to be anything really onerous in the covenants, if indeed there are any at all. But to keep up the myth that house ownership is very complicated, it will be surprising if some legal genius along the line hasn't slipped a few covenants in just to make himself feel more at home. But for the general run of houses bought and sold by the general run of people, what are the covenants that are likely to turn up? They fall into a pattern and the commonest are:-

1. Not to use the house for any trade or business.

2. To keep a fence or fences in repair either by yourself or with the assistance of your neighbour.

3. Not to build another house on the plot or extend the present one without permission of some previous owner.

4. If you build a house on the plot it must be of at least £x in value.

5. Not to do anything to cause a nuisance.

So if you find any or all of 1-5 in either the Charge Certificate or in the copy of covenants etc. which comes with the Charge Certificate, how do you interpret them for your own purposes? If you are sufficiently irreverent you have no doubt already cracked the code for yourself. Irreverence is the key to DIY conveyancing. A refusal to be showered with *bovinus excrementus* is a sure shield against loss of confidence. However:

1. So what? You are buying the house to live in.

2. Probably nothing could be done, as money would have to be spent to enforce it.

3. Put it this way: if the house has a double garden and you were buying with the idea of putting a little bungalow on for your granny, you would ask the vendor to put you in touch with the previous vendor who put the restriction on. Ten to one he can't, because the previous owner will turn out to be Mr. Wraith, and there is but the ghost of a chance of finding anyone of his kith or kin who either know or care about the covenant. So you could go ahead and be ninety-nine per cent certain you were safe. There are even Insurance companies who will, for a modest sum, indemnify you against that one per

cent risk of someone turning up and trying to make trouble.

4. As at (3) above. You might ask Mr. Skinner if he can produce evidence that the house you are buying actually cost that amount to build, but you are unlikely to receive much of a reply unless it is something in the nature of "there is no builder's receipt in the deeds but the vendor has received no notice of breach of covenant."

5. Other people might think that we cause nuisance, but we know that it is they who cause nuisance. They are wrong and we are right, but perverse as always, they think they know best. So we can accept this covenant because firstly, we never cause nuisance and secondly, we have an ordinary common law obligation, like everybody else, not to cause nuisance anyway.

Covenants are promises and the only difference between a covenant and any other kind of promise is that it is contained in a deed. At some point in the history of the buying and selling of the land in question, some owner has said in effect to some anxious buyer, "I will only sell to you if you will promise this that and the other, and also promise that when you sell, you will have your buyer make the same promise to me, and so on ad infinitum".

There are two important things to be said about this ruling-from-the-grave covenanting. Firstly, many a covenant is so imprecise that it is difficult to say if it is or ever was enforceable, and secondly, it is difficult to say who could enforce it anyway. In general it is difficult, if not impossible to enforce a covenant that is expressed to be simply in favour of a person without reference to land he owns or owned.

If you come across a "no building or extension" covenant in the charges register of a property you are thinking of buying, and your inspection of the property has shown the covenant to have been broken, what do you do about it? The first thing to ascertain is how long the extension or building has stood there. In addition to the owner's say-so ask for some independent evidence from him. If the building is more than a few years old, however, you can be pretty sure that even if the covenant were precise and was capable of enforcement the fact that at the time of building, and immediately subsequent to it, no objection was raised, means the covenant in question would be deemed to have been waived. If you are the owner, you can put the potential purchaser's mind at rest by offering to insure him against the risk for say ten years. If you are the purchaser you can pull a long face and say that but for your spouse's silly emotional feeling for the place, you would have cried off immediately, and you will now do so unless a few pounds are knocked off the price agreed before you knew about this diabolical covenant. Having got the reduction agreed, you get the insurance — if you feel it is really necessary; and that's the dead hand of the past contained in any entries in Section C of the Office Copies dealt with.

Entries No. 3 and 4 in the Charges Register have been struck out, and as the legend at the foot of the page has it, any entries struck through are no longer subsisting — exactly, they are dead.

Entries No. 5 and 6 refer to the present owner's mortgage. "Charge" is an abbreviation of "Legal Charge" and "Legal Charge" is the fancy term for "mortgage".

In our example we have not been able to cover all the things that might be entered on a Charges Register. For instance, Smart's building society might not like a second mortgage to be entered unless they know about it so you get "no disposition of the property may be made without the consent of the proprietor of Charge No......" Don't worry, the Building Society won't let go without their money, so their charge will be deleted when you come to register. There might be something about Capital Transfer Tax monies having to come out of the proceeds of the sale on the death of Mr. Croakes. Don't worry, it's nothing to do with you, it's Croakes's executor's problem.

OFFICE COPY

H.M. LAND REGISTRY

TITLE NUMBER EDN999707

This register consists of 6 *pages*

Edition 1
opened 16.3.67

A. PROPERTY REGISTER

containing the description of the registered land and the estate comprised in the Title

TITLE NUMBER

ADMINISTRATIVE AREA	PARISH OR PLACE
EDENSHIRE	BLOSSOMTON

The Freehold land shown and edged with red on the plan of the above Title
filed at the Registry registered on 16th March, 1967 known as 14 Plevna Place,
Blossomton Parish together with rights granted by but subject to the
exceptions and reservations contained in the transfer dated 6th January, 1972
referred to in Entry No.2 of the Charges Register.

page . 2.

B. PROPRIETORSHIP REGISTER

TITLE NUMBER EDN999707

stating nature of the Title, name, address and description of the proprietor of the land and any entries affecting the right of disposing thereof

TITLE ABSOLUTE

Entry number	Proprietor, etc.	Remarks
1.	~~BRIAN FEATHER and PAULINE FEATHER both of 14 Plevna Place, Blossomton, registered 14th February, 1972~~	~~£5,000 Price paid~~
2.	CLINT SMART and CONSTANCE SMART both of 14 Plevna Place, Blossomton, registered 16th November, 1977	

Any entries struck through are no longer subsisting

DISTRICT LAND REGISTRY SHOWING THE SUBSISTING ENTRIES ON THE REGISTER ON | 3 | OCT | 1978

Another really irritating one is where there is an entry that the land is subject to covenants set out in a deed dated the umpteenth of Nerth. In the remarks column you then read "deed not lodged with registry". If at first and subsequent registrations nobody bothered to protect their interests by telling the Registry what the covenants were, it is extremely unlikely they ever will. Ignore it.

You're not really reading a detective story for fun so you are allowed to see how Mr. Newman's story concludes in the case where you come across the real mother and father of Rigmarole in, or referred to in the Property Register, and it starts off about Sewers and unmade roads and rights across them, — *skip to the end*. Ten to one you will find that the rigmarole was inserted as a condition of planning permission being granted for the estate to be built. Once the house was completed and its drains connected with the main sewer in the road, and the council had taken over responsibility for maintenance of the road (it had become a highway) and the sewer, the rigmarole was of academic interest only, except insofar as all subsequent inspectors of Office Copies have, at least, to give it a quick glance.

It is unlikely that you will come up against a Caution. Like many other terms and phrases in the lawyers' armoury, "caution" has an ominous ring to it, so let us cut it down to size before the few readers to whom it might apply are faced with it. Cautions are, almost without exception, hostile. That is because a caution is used where the owner of the property will not co-operate with a person who requires protection of his or her interests. You will be extremely unlucky to come up against a caution, but if you do, in nine hundred and ninety nine cases out of a thousand, the vendor will already know about it, and as he wants his sale to you to go through, will already have made arrangements for the caution to be removed.

The most common caution you are likely to see entered nowadays is one by a wife who wishes to let all who are interested to purchase know that though the house was not bought in joint names it is, in fact, the matrimonial home. By registering the caution she makes sure that if her husband tries to

OFFICE COPY

C. CHARGES REGISTER

containing charges, incumbrances, etc., adversely affecting the land and registered dealings therewith

Page 3 3

TITLE NUMBER EDN999707

Entry number	The date at the beginning of each entry is the date on which the entry was made on this edition of the register.	Remarks
1.	16th March, 1967 A conveyance of the land in this title dated 27th January, 1967 made between Thomas Dick Vendor and Charles Harry purchaser, contains the following covenants. "The purchaser for the benefit of the remainder of the vendors land hereby covenants with the Vendor to the intent that the burden of this covenant may run with and bind the land hereby conveyed to observe and perform the stipulations and restrictions set out in the schedule hereto. THE SCHEDULE before referred to: 1. No further building shall be erected on the said land without the consent of the Vendor. 2. Not at any time to carry on or suffer to be carried on the said land any trade or business for the sale of intoxicating liquors and no building erected on the said land shall be used except as a private dwelling house.	
2.	14th February, 1972 A transfer dated 31st January, 1972 by Sunshine Investments Ltd. to Brian Feather and Pauline Feather contains restrictive convenants (Copy in Certificate)	Copy in Certificate
3.	~~14th February 1972 CHARGE dated 31st January, 1972 registered on 14th February, 1972 to secure the monies therein mention.~~	
4.	~~PROPRIETOR WOOLWICH EQUITABLE BUILDING SOCIETY registered 14th February, 1972.~~	
5.	16th November, 1977 – CHARGE dated 1st November, 1977 registered on 16th November, 1977 to secure the monies including the further advances therein mentioned.	
6.	PROPRIETOR – Heart of England Building Society Jury Street, Warwick, registered 16th November, 1977	

GAINSBOROUGH DR

Plevna Place

Any entries struck through in red are no longer subsisting

sell the house, she will get to know about it and can be on the spot for a division of the proceeds. She may also have entered the caution to make sure her husband doesn't take further mortgages without her consent. Another caution is one against first registration, and this device is sometimes used where deeds have been handed over on security for a loan, and the lender does not trust the borrower not to make a sale and pretend he has lost the deeds. It will be an extremely rare case where the reply to your Form 96 (application for an official search of the index map) shows a caution against first registration. Any type of caution entitles the cautioner to be notified of any proposed dealings.

A prospective purchaser who finds a caution on the register will quite rightly ask the vendor to have it removed by clearing up whatever problem exists between himself and the cautioner. A caution against dealing can be withdrawn at any time without fee, using Form 71. The vendor will either persuade the cautioner to write to the Registrar asking for the removal of the caution (Form 71) from the register, or if the vendor knows the caution to be simply silly and vexatious, he himself can apply for its removal. He must do one or the other or both. The Registrar then gives the cautioner notice of the proposed dealing, and informs him that he intends to remove the caution. The onus is then on the cautioner to take action and if he doesn't make a serious objection within fourteen days after notification, the caution is cancelled. The caution has been "warned off". When he hears from the Registrar, the cautioner may, if he wishes, put his case to him. The Registrar has a wide discretion, and he can, after hearing both sides, do what he thinks appropriate, i.e. remove the caution from the register; refuse to let the proposed dealing proceed; allow the proposed dealing to proceed, but subject in some way to the cautioner's interest; give a time limit within which the cautioner must institute legal proceedings or have the caution removed. All the Registrar's discretionary decisions in these instances are subject to appeal in the courts.

Now note the difference between the date when the charge (mortgage) was signed, 1st November, 1977, and the date when it was registered, also the difference between the date of the transfer from Sunshine to Feather (31st January) noted at Charge 2 and the registering of that transfer on the Proprietorship Register (14th February). During those time lags, you say to yourself, the house could have been sold to half-a-dozen others. Don't panic! This all brings us to an explanation of what the significance and usefulness of the date stamped in the right-hand corner of each sheet of the Office Copies represents. Sometimes, what are sent from solicitors and look like office copies, are not, — they are photo-copies that Skinner, Tight and Wadd have taken from office copies, and could be years out of date, — so watch that date stamp.

That date stamp tells you when the copy in our case, 3rd October 1978, was taken from the actual register. Office Copies come to you from the Registry by First Class Post, but even so they are obviously out of date by the time you are proving to yourself how simple it all is by glancing through the entries. On the 4th October the Smarts could have sold the house to Mr. G. A. Zump and he could have registered the transfer to him on the 5th October, 1978 before you have time to do anything about it. Here you are with a copy of the register which clearly shows Smarts as the owners on the 3rd October — how could one possibly stop the ubiquitous Mr. Zump? There is a way, and again it is a form, green in colour and 94A by number. You will meet it again later and be properly introduced.

At the bottom of the example Office Copy Charges Register, I have appended a typical plan of "the Freehold Land shown and edged with red" that is filed on the register. Note the scale. Note the thickness of the lines which delineate the boundaries, and what width of real land they cover and represent. Make a note not to get steamed up or get involved with those who get steamed up about who owns which six inches of the blessed plot, that is, unless you have a private sea of silver to let lawyers go trawling in.

Legal opinion

Britain is not yet as lawyer-ridden as the United States and, to a lesser extent, West Germany. But evidently lawyers have improved their status and fortunes a good deal here since the days of Sir Henri Deterding, the founder of Royal Dutch/ **Shell.**

In a letter dated September 13, 1916, which has—as investigative reports say—come into my possession, Sir Henri sharply rebuked his Managing Director in New York, Mr. Luyks, for making excessive use of lawyers' services.

"Although we have an enormous business here", Sir Henri wrote, "we very rarely consult lawyers . . . lawyers are not business people. However large a lawyer's experience may be, in the conduct of business he is absolutely useless. A lawyer placed at the head of a concern would soon bring the business to rack and ruin.

" . . . to ask his opinion as to what you should do or not do is the worst possible way of conducting business, which should be kept as far as possible from the lawyers.

"We do not wish a lawyer to give his entire time to our business", says Sir Henri firmly. "We have not got daily disputes, neither do we wish to create them. A lawyer . . . . is to give us advice if trouble arises, and if you employ him, say six times a year, this can be considered the average maximum . . . I hate to see a lawyer in our office. If I want him I go to *his* office and limit the conversation to the shortest possible time." Would that this robust spirit still blew through the corridors of British management!

Roger Berthoud

'The Times', 13.3.80

10. Doing
Your Own
Conveyance

Having learned about mortgages, contracts, restrictive covenants and the registration of property you are now ready to do your own conveyance. While reading what follows keep the appropriate flow diagram by your side, and ignoring what you were told when you first learned to read, trace the action out with your index finger as you go.

There is, of course a lot that is slightly technical which you might have to read twice before you think that you have grasped the point. You will certainly, as with any technical instruction, find that understanding comes the quicker when instead of just the printed page you have the actual nuts and bolts of the job in front of you. Every time you wire an electric plug it becomes easier — it's the same with conveyancing.

In the days when a solicitor could act for both parties even if he had never acted for them before, I met an aged gentleman who was selling a house he had lived in for over thirty years. When he was asked who his solicitor was, he said quite simply "I don't need a solicitor. I own the house, the deeds are under the piano lid, and when I get my money, the buyer can have keys, house and deeds, and I'm off into a Home with the proceeds." I gave him a receipt for the Deeds and took them to Donald Turnbull, solicitor for the purchaser, who, being the wise old bird he was, made no fuss and got on with it. After all, what had he to do? He looked at the last conveyance in the pile, made sure that the purchaser therein named was the aged gentleman, and bingo, aged gent had proved title. (It is even simpler and safer nowadays where we have registered title). A month later the old boy was ensconced in the Home terrorising the Matron with his merciless logic.

So if you have got your house paid for, follow the example of aged gent, by getting your deeds. Whether your house is paid for or not get *the whole file of your purchase transaction* from the solicitor who acted for you years ago, (as you are fully entitled to it, having paid his bill), and pop the papers under your own piano lid to be ready. As you take your first confident step keep firmly in mind that you are out to achieve three things: (1) Save yourself at the very least £120: that's for a sale. It's a whole lot more if you buy as well. (2) Get the purchase price safely out of the buyer's pocket and into yours. (3) Make certain you are completely shot of the house and have no continuing liabilities which you do by virtue of Clause 4 in our model Contract. To save the £120 requires that you read on: the second only requires that you are numerate and can count the money in banknotes or recognise a banker's draft for the same sum. You may have jibbed just a tiny bit at the third. Don't — just think of the hassle, worry and money you're about to save yourself. In any case, even if you pay a solicitor you will, no doubt have to do most of the running about yourself.

You can do without dragging yourself down town to the office of that well-known and aptly named legal expert Mr. Skinner and competing for his attention against a continuous barrage of telephone interruptions, just to be told that Mr. Skinner is saving you from being left with continuing liabilities after you have sold by telling you to get the meters read on the day you leave. Nine times out of ten it will be left to you to tell the Rating Authority to send their demands to someone else. So you see, whether you pay Mr. Skinner's fees or do-it-yourself you will in fact end up doing a lot of the work yourself.

Selling a Registered House

Whether you intend to travel fifty yards or fifty miles, your journey begins with a single step. You may not know whether you can walk fifty yards let alone fifty miles, but you have not much to lose by risking one stride, and emboldened by the success of that one stride you will not lack confidence for the next two. So let me give you, the layman conveyancer, the confidence to take that first stride by explaining step by step how to complete the simplest of all housing transactions, that of selling a second hand freehold registered house in England or Wales which is free of mortgage.

How little of a "legal" nature there is to do you will see from the step by step table at the end of the chapter. Step No. 1 is to get out your Land Certificate and copy the title number onto Land Registry form A44, Application for Office Copies (obtainable from H.M.S.O.) add your name & address, tick the box marked "complete set", attach a cheque (or Land Registry stamps obtainable from the Post Office) value £2.25p* and post it off to the appropriate Land Registry which you will find in Appendix I. In seven to ten days you will receive a set of copies of everything carried on the Land Register about your house.

While waiting for the office copies to come from the the Land Registry spend a few minutes making up three copies of the contract as per sample on page 53, keep one copy for your file and put the other two, with the office copies, when you receive them, into an envelope, addressed to the purchaser's solicitor, Mr. Skinner, with a covering letter telling him that you are acting for yourself in the sale of your house to Mr. Feather (purchaser).

Mr. Skinner will write back acknowledging receipt, and, as though he had never heard of such a thing before, he will ask you to confirm that you are indeed acting for yourself. In return for your confirmation he will send you a letter giving the game away that he knew all the time that people are doing their own conveyancing nowadays. And he will put the evidence of his clever dickery on paper: he will say he must make it clear that he will "take no responsibility for

*1983: £3

you in law or otherwise." He might even, as some do, say he is giving the warning in accordance with a Law Society directive. If he does he is lying. There is no such directive. There was a mention of the problem in the Lawyers' journal but that is all. Think about it! If it weren't becoming the in thing to do one's own conveyancing, why has the editorial staff of the Law Society's journal had to sit down in solemn conclave to decide how to advise their members about how to cope with the phenomenon?

There is no kind of business in the land that isn't regulated by general and particular laws which protect those with whom they deal. Nobody can write themselves out of the law, and nobody should know that better than Mr. Skinner. What "or otherwise" means I simply do not know — you try asking. I've never managed to get a sensible excuse, let alone an explanation. Though you might feel like writing in retaliation, it is best to take no notice, as you have already landed a left and a right, where it hurts him most, in the pride and in the pocket.

You now receive from Mr. Skinner an 'Enquiries before Contract' form. This form is covered in questions. But it is different from an examination paper, because you only have to answer those questions to which you are absolutely certain you know the answers. If you don't know the answers or are not certain about them, you calmly ask the examiner to check up for himself by replying "not as far as I am aware but please make own enquiries", or quite simply "I don't know". At first reading, the form may appear quite fearsome. But really it is quite straightforward, if you keep firmly fixed in your head that you don't intend giving any hostages to fortune, and you intend cleaving to the old-established precept of "caveat emptor", which is Latin for "let the buyer beware". If you are a buyer reading this, N.B.

Mr. Skinner asks you about the fearsome-sounding liabilities, covenants, easements, rights or informal arrangements, grants, wayleaves, licenses, consents and restrictions that might or might not appear on your Land Certificate. Note he is using a printed form. He hasn't had the wet towels cooling the brow fevered by worry for his client's safety. A vendor simply shuffles any restrictions, covenants, etc. onto the purchaser. The solicitor who acted for the man who sold your house to you did it to you — and your solicitor let him. And why? Because there is nothing you or any solicitor breathing can do about the covenants etc. at this stage. They go with the property, are registered at the Land Registry and that is that. As a matter of fact, you have already dealt with that little lot by including my suggested clause 4 in your contract and in reply to these enquiries from the purchaser you just keep on using ritual phrases based on "The property is sold subject to any covenants, liabilities, etc. there may be". In the parcel under the piano lid you might have the similar form your solicitor received from the vendor's solicitor when you bought. From that you will see how little a solicitor gets in response to his enquiries before contract intended to protect his client in the parlous procedures entailed in the biggest business operation of his client's life. "To the best of my knowledge, no, but please rely on your own searches". "I don't know". "There may be, but never brought to my attention". These are the kind of woolly replies to expect to woolly questions.

The same "Enquiries before Contract" also asks you if there is any dry rot in the house, where the main drains run, and such things as how long since the Electricity Board tested the supply. I've even been asked, "Is the road fronting the property a public highway?" when I knew that Mr. Skinner whizzed past in his car every day, that is, unless he was halted in his progress by a double-decker bus which did a request stop by the gate. So give these questions the same treatment as above. In answer to "What is the Rateable Value?" blandly reply with the Rateable Value from your rates bill but tag on "......but please check with local council". There will no doubt be a question (the content of the form changes from time to time) about facilities shared in common. If you know of a shared drive, hedge or wall, say so, but don't be bullied about it — there are seldom any supporting documents about such things. If you have built a garage since you bought, say so, and offer a copy of the plans. But if you are asked, "were all planning laws and restrictions complied with?" duck your head down into the trench again with "I think so, but please enquire of local planning dept." Whatever questions you are asked, don't let them put the breeze up you. Remember, conveyancing is an administrative, business transaction, and only becomes judicial when fraud etc. raises its ugly head. In any case, you are not replying to the Solicitor General, or the Lord Chancellor, or, in most cases, a solicitor even, but to a clerk in a solicitor's office.

You will also be asked when possession of the property will be given. You answer, "When I receive the balance of the money by Banker's Draft on completion which will take place at (state a venue convenient to you)." Avoid the completion taking place at Mr. Skinner's office, as, true to his profession, he will try to lord it over you. (If you are also buying a house you may wish to add a suggested completion date to tie in with your purchase, but see Chapter 8 for more on this subject). It takes some believing, but this is the right way to deal with the Enquiries before Contract, and Skinner's acceptance of your answers will be your proof. However, if Skinner is in stroppy mood, he could pick on some answer you have given and ask you to be more specific. If he does, and you simply don't know the answer, just stick at it, saying you have nothing to add. If he really does seem to be giving you the run-around, consider the possibility that he knows the proposed purchaser has gone off, and he is indulging himself with a D.I.Y. conveyancer and attempting to bring him to his knees. If you suspect this, check up with the purchaser direct. Though solicitors consider it unethical for one solicitor to speak with another solicitor's client, there is no law, rule or ethic on earth that prevents the two principals (in this case vendor and purchaser) discussing matters between themselves.

When Skinner has accepted your replies to Enquiries before Contract he will approve your contract, have Feather sign it, and send it back to you. You now need to collect the deposit and hand over your signed contract. If you have arranged that your bank manager or someone else will act as stakeholder repair to his office and exchange the contract you have signed for the one signed by the purchaser, and see to it that the balance of the deposit is handed to the stakeholder. Your sale is now tied up. If the buyer backs out, you have to decide whether to be merciful or merciless. That is to say you give him back all, part or none of his deposit, depending on the circumstances.

After exchange of contracts, Skinner may send a questionnaire entitled "Requisition on Title". If he does, treat it with olympian calm. Requisition means question. Title means ownership. So he is asking you questions to find out if you are the owner when all the time you know and he knows you are the owner because it says so on the Land Registry Proprietorship Register, and your title (ownership) is thus guaranteed by the State. What more does he want? Jam on it? They keep changing the form so you may get questions raising problems which have already been solved, like where completion will take place, and have you got receipts for rates and such like bills paid. I know it's difficult, but try to be courteous, remembering all the while that even if you were paying a solicitor, all these problems would still be yours to solve.

Mr. Skinner, on behalf of your purchaser Mr. Feather now sends you a Land Registry Form 19 in draft state for your approval. This is the form which authorises the Land Registry to transfer the house out of your ownership into Mr. Feather's. If the draft is in order, and it can scarcely be otherwise, as it only calls for names and addresses to be filled in, accept it and write acknowledging the fact. Sign Form 19 (both of you, if in joint names), have it witnessed and hold on to it. There is nothing to do now but while away the time before completion date by dreaming about what you will spend the money on.

Sometimes purchasers will ask you to let them have the keys before completion. If Mr. Feather needs to get the money from the sale of his own house to Mr. Dither in order to buy yours it can be difficult for him. But if Dither gets knocked down by a bus on his way to complete, and you have let Feather into possession of your house, it will be a great deal more difficult for you. If you are selling a vacant property you will no doubt be asked to accept an undertaking from Mr. Feather that if you let him have the key solely for the purpose of decorating and repairing, he will not go into possession. Now it might seem a bit dog-in-the-manger to refuse, and his solicitor Mr. Skinner at his pontifical best will assure you that it is the usual thing, and the undertaking he has drafted for Mr. Feather to sign gives you ample protection. If you feel under pressure, write to Mr. Skinner and ask for his personal indemnity underwriting the Feathers' undertaking. You never know, he might give it. But if he can't trust his own client, how can you?

If the buyer is all tied up at his end and cannot attend the completion personally, leave the keys with a neighbour you can trust. A further qualification to being trustworthy that the neighbour requires is that he be on the telephone, because on pain of having to support Coventry City A.F.C. for the rest of his natural life, he must not hand over the keys until you have rung up telling him to do so.

On completion day toddle along to the appointed venue. You will have with you your Land Certificate, the completed Form 19 and the keys (if not with neighbour). If the deposit is being held by your estate agent and his office is not the venue for completion Mr. Skinner will in addition to handing you the balance of the purchase price, give you a letter authorising the stakeholder to hand over the deposit. You give Mr. Skinner the Land Certificate, Form 19 and the keys. And that is your sale completed.

Here are the ten steps to be taken when selling a registered house in England and Wales. If you spend more than one and a half hours filling in the forms etc. — you are a slacker.

1. Send form A44 to the Land Registry.

2. Send two copies of a draft contract to purchaser together with office copies and authority to inspect register.

3. Receive Enquiries before Contract.

4. Send replies.

5. Exchange his signed contract for yours and receive Requisitions on Title.

6. Reply to Requisitions on Title.

7. Receive transfer Form 19 in draft.

8. Approve.

9. Collect the money, and hand over signed Form 19, Land Certificate and keys.

10. Feel very proud of yourself, not because of the difficult task you have accomplished, but because you had the courage to overcome all the hogwash propaganda that has persuaded house owners that they needed highly qualified legal brains to do their conveyancing for them.

10a. Receive praise of relatives and friends who will be coming round in the hope of free drinks from the money you saved by doing it yourself.

11. Doing the Sale and Purchase of a Registered House

The earlier chapter on selling a registered house confined itself to the work a vendor of such a house is faced with. The reason for limiting its scope was so that the reader could judge for himself the simplicity of the operation. Indeed, anyone who is good at making a précis will have already noted that a very simple transaction indeed could be carried out and it goes like this:

A purchaser goes to the front door of a house that is for sale and says, "I will give you £20,000 for this edifice provided you can prove to me that you are the owner of what you say you are." The proud owner says "Done, come back in a couple of hours with the folding money". The purchaser returns with the money and confirms that the vendor has loaded a furniture van with his belongings and the house is cleared. The vendor is clutching his Land Certificate and a Form of Transfer No. 19 in one hand and the keys in the other. The purchaser swaps his £20,000 for the Land Certificate, Transfer Form and keys and the deal is done. The purchaser sends the Land Certificate and the Transfer to the Land Registry and he is now the registered proprietor.

Because people tend not to take other people's word for

things nowadays it takes a bit longer than this, but basically what appears above is the beginning and end of a sale and purchase of registered land. It contains everything that has to be done to transfer ownership.

The instructions that follow are for the purchase and sale of a freehold second-hand house in England or Wales which is already registered. The instructions should also be read in conjunction with Chapter 7 regarding contracts. For the purpose of illustration we will assume that you are a first time buyer and need to take a mortgage, or that you are the vendor of a £20,000 house. There is some repetition of what has gone earlier — unfortunately it cannot be avoided so please look on it as part of the teaching and learning process.

Vendor As soon as you seriously put your house up for sale send off an Application for Office Copies Form A44 obtainable from H.M.S.O.. Fill in your name and address and Title number, which you have got from your Land Certificate, your Building Society or the solicitor who acted for you when you bought (he cannot charge you for this little service, by rights he should have performed it earlier) and tick the box ordering "complete set". Attach Registry stamps to the value of £2.25p* and send it off to the appropriate Land Registry which you can track down in Appendix I.

Purchaser Until you are sure you can find the money for the purchase, sign nothing, apart from the Building Society's application form. Any letters you send to anyone must have written somewhere about them "Subject to Contract" and it is safest to keep on doing that right up to the point where you do sign the contract. I take it for granted that you will keep your wits about you, and have at some time completed a licence or passport application form, and have, therefore, clerical expertise. That little caution given, I will not labour the points that are usually made ad infinitum and ad nauseam elsewhere, about how careful one must be. I wouldn't mind, if such labourings genuinely helped people either towards a better understanding, or to being able to cope for themselves and ease

*1983: £3

their worries, but when, after scaring the living daylights out of you, the only advice given is: go to a professional to deal with a contract for you, survey for you, buy for you, sell for you, it's just a waste of reading time. You can always leave things to others — at a price — and people had to when they were illiterate. One cardinal rule, and it goes for all business transactions, is: never let go of both ends. Have the house, or have the money. The cynic would say, preferably have both, but never be in the position where you have neither.

Before committing yourself to anything, re-read the section on contracts because the vendor whose heart you warmed with those magic words, "I would like to buy your house", has been on the phone to Skinner and gleefully told him that he has found a buyer and Skinner says "Leave it all to me". What, at this point, Feather has left to him is the sending on of a draft contract and that is what in the fullness of time you can expect to receive, but he might also write to you as he did to our D.I.Y. vendor in the previous chapter, saying that he won't be responsible to you in law or otherwise. If he does, join in the fun by ringing up his client (Mr. Feather) and ask what Skinner is covering up — what is wrong with the house, is it down for road widening, is there a deed missing, has he got the scrolls or hasn't he? —- plus any further nonsense *you* can think up. Then forget about it.

Vendor Send off to the purchaser's solicitor two copies of your draft contract and the office copies which you should have received by now, together with an authority to inspect the register. If you know which Building Society your purchaser is getting his mortgage from, send an authority for them in addition. See page 64 for suggested draft.

Purchaser Receive draft contract and possibly office copies. Not all solicitors are as obliging as our do-it-yourself vendor and at this stage they only send an authority to inspect the register. If you only get an authority never mind, pin it to an Application for Office Copies form A44 on which you have written the title number* address of the property to be purchased, your own name and address clearly in the box for "person to whom the office copies are to be sent", tick box for Complete Set and stick on £2.25p† Land Registry stamps and send the lot off to the appropriate Land Registry which you will find in the Appendix. If your vendor's solicitors are Skinner, Tight and Wadd whom we met earlier when they were saving a pound or two by producing their own "office copies" by putting Land or Charge Certificates through their own photo-copier, take note of two things, — 1: That the number of pages they send corresponds with the number printed at the top right hand corner of the Property Register, and 2: that the date printed in the box at the bottom right hand corner is recent. If you are not absolutely satisfied with what you get, ask for an authority to apply direct for your own up to date copies.

Either office copies or an authority to inspect are accept-able from the vendor's solicitor, but he might send neither. Solicitors tend to divide conveyancing into two parts as to work done before contract and from contract to completion. This was understandable in the days before registered property proliferated, and when photo-copiers hadn't yet become part of every reasonably well-equipped office, but to continue in such a vein seems to be rooted in an inability to change. So if Skinner, Standing and Still send neither office copies nor authority to inspect, insist on one or the other. In either, or any case, peruse the office copies in the light of the knowledge you gained from the Chapter "The Registers".

Put the draft contract on one side for a little while and content yourself with sending two copies of Enquiries Before Contract form CON 29 (long) obtainable from OYEZ publications to the vendor's solicitor. Before you do, have a quick look through it, and if the questions it contains don't cover everything you would like to ask about, and hopefully get a sensible answer to, add those questions to the form under the heading "Additional Enquiries". For instance, buyers of new houses should ask, "Is the design, construction and layout of the sewers such as will meet the criteria required for their adoption by the water and any other authority?"

---

*Given to you in second paragraph of contract as on p.53.
†1983: £3

Vendors now have to deal with the form "Enquiries before Contract" and *Purchasers* can look over their shoulders. Indeed, anyone who has not coped with these enquiries before will do well to have his seconds ready in his corner for this form will be the one that will (at first) make you wish you had never bothered, that is, until you have really started pencilling in some replies in the copy which is intended for you to keep. As you read on and pencil away, the colour will come back to your cheeks, and you will realise how childish it was to be frightened.

The form asks fifteen questions on Freehold Property and there is space for the purchaser to include more questions of his own devising. Most of the questions are easy, daft, or both, but we will have a quick run down them all, first noting that the column headed "Replies" already has displayed in bold type "These replies on behalf of the vendor are believed to be correct but the accuracy is not guaranteed and they do not obviate the need to make appropriate searches, enquiries and inspections."* Questions 1 and 2 relate to boundaries and whether you know of any disputes about them. If you know the answers, give them, if you are not sure, use the formula "I know of none" and give the same answer to Question 3, particularly insofar as it refers to your predecessors in the house.

Question 4(a) asks for copies of any Housebuilding Council guarantee, Insurance Policies covering defective title, or road maintenance agreements. If you have any, comply, if not, you can't, so just reply "none in my possession". 4(b) asks if you've claimed under any of the agreements at 4(a) and how you got on. Question 5 asks about services such as gas, electricity, water and drains connected, and if the service comes to you through someone else's property. The first part is easy, the second is easier when you know how. Answer: "Please rely on your own survey". Deal with Questions 6 and 7 about access and roads in a similar fashion. Question 8(a) is about rights of way again. If you know of any, say so, if not, say "I am not aware". 8(b) could frighten you out of your wits and send you scurrying off for legal help. Don't

---

*Nevertheless, the law on misrepresentation still applies, as should the good old British principle "my word is my bond".

let either happen. It asks "Is the vendor aware of any other over-riding interests as defined by the Land Registration Acts 1925 S 70(1)?" Take a deep breath and write in "This question is far too broad. Please be more specific." This answer has always sufficed in my experience. But just in case you need to know, you can find section 70(1) of the Land Registration Act 1925 printed on the inside cover of the Land Certificate if your house is paid for, or at page 38 in "Wontner's Land Registry Practice" by F. Quickfall published by OYEZ publications. The overriding interests referred to occupy about a page and a half. Mr. Skinner is trying with Question 8(b) to make sure that when Feather dies, his widow will not see his best beast siezed and led away by his lord, nor will Feather, during his lifetime be liable to repair the chancel of the church. If Mr. Skinner does come back with specific questions about profits à prendre, watercourses, quit-rents, scrotage and the like, tell him you've never heard such words before in all your life, and to watch his language.

Having answered 8(b) you've broken its back. It's downhill all the way now and you can answer the remaining questions with variations on our old friend "I don't know of any, but please rely on your own survey." Even with the question about Rateable Value, even though you have the latest rate bill sitting in front of you, it is safest, and perfectly acceptable to reply "I think £xxxx but please check with local authority."

Even though you have specified the fitted wardrobes, shelving and such like in a final clause of your contract, this doesn't stop the question cropping up again at Question 11. You will find this kind of duplicate questioning happening all the time. I'm afraid you just have to put up with it and give it the short shrift it deserves. Question 13 asks how long after the exchange of contracts will the Vendor be able to give vacant possession. It may be perfectly possible for you to give possession the next day, but the usual period is one month. So give a date which you think is suitable to the purchaser and also make it clear where and how you insist on having

the money, e.g. "Vacant possession will be given on completion
which will take place at (state venue) on the umpteenth of
Nerth. A bankers' draft will be required for the balance of
the purchase price." (A cheque could bounce)

"Enquiries before Contract" having been completed to
your satisfaction, send it off to the purchaser or the solicitor
who is acting for him. He may come back with supplementary
questions, and some of them may appear to be intended to
annoy you or even make you despair. Don't let annoyance
creep in, or despair push you into doing anything silly with
your money, like giving it to a solicitor, just press on, courteously pointing out that you can only sell what you have got,
but you are not a qualified surveyor and if he wants to be
absolutely certain where such things as the drains run, he is
welcome to have a sniff around provided he does no damage.

Purchasers: Receive the Enquiries before Contract series LM
Con 29 (Long) completed, and glean from it what you can.
Though we made fun of Question 8(b) on behalf of our vendor
dealing with a solicitor do be careful that as a purchaser
the laugh is not on you, because under Section 70 (1) (g)
it is now possible for someone, apart from the registered
proprietor, to claim rights of occupation (and the courts will
not shift them), even though they have not registered that
right anywhere except as an animal does by leaving its scent
at the site.

So at the risk of repetition you will find throughout this
book endless warnings about making sure before you sign
a contract that the vendor *can* give you vacant possession on
completion, and NEVER EVER complete the purchase of a
house before you have seen with your own eyes that the house
is completely vacated, and that if there has been any kind of
dispute about ownership and/or occupation, that the locks
have been changed. If you think you may gain further enlight-
enment by asking supplementaries, ask them, but remember
they were stock questions, so you couldn't expect much more
than stock answers. Better still, make a trip to the property
and using the form as a check list, go through the items with

the Vendor. If after reading this book you think the job beyond your powers and decide to employ a solicitor, *I strongly urge you to read the following and carry out the inspection recommended because if you don't, nobody else will!* Paying a dog and barking yourself? Well, to coin the football manager's phrase, "That's what it's all about, isn't it?" In many cases that is how some vendors and purchasers often feel about matters even when they have instructed solicitors to act for them, and find themselves doing the work.

Have a look at the boundaries, walls, fences with your own eyes. The general run of houses, detached, semi and terraced in town and suburban areas have clearly defined garden walls, hedges and fences, but in the rural areas it isn't always so. However, first check what is within the boundaries with the plan. If there is more within the fences than the plan shows, it is possible that your vendor has pinched it. Ask him about it. Ask the neighbour. If there is a problem, it isn't too much trouble to move a fence, but what about a garage? Always check that a garage is within the boundary shown on your plan. Indications that there may be some dispute about boundaries, or whose responsibility it is to maintain a particular fence, could be evidenced by its broken-down nature. If you have any reason to suspect that there is any kind of dispute about a boundary, fence, or worst of all a shared drive, go hot foot to the neighbour and ask his point of view about it.

In my experience, disputes between owner-occupiers of suburban properties about who owns what and who can go where are the most frustrating, intractable, time-consuming and above all ruinously costly to resolve at law. If you come across a hint of such a dispute, my advice is, run a mile. Hard lines on the vendor, who hasn't had the courage or foresight to come to terms with his neighbour; *his* best hope is that his prospective purchaser has not read this book and that the whole business is being conducted at arm's length by solicitors: the vendor using a solicitor in John O'Groats where he is buying his new house and the purchaser using a solicitor in the area he is moving to the Midlands from — Land's End.

If in order to get to the house or garage you have to

traverse an unmade road, or anything that looks as if it may
not be a public right of way (and the council will tell you
if it is in reply to your enquiry form — see p. 96) there should
be a note on the Office Copy saying you have a right of way
over the track or common drive or whatever. On the other hand
does anyone else have a right of way over land which is shown,
on the plan, to be that which you are contemplating buying, and
if so, are they the neighbourly type?

.If the copy of the deed plan which came as part of the
Register has produced no satisfactory answer about the approach to the property, ask the vendor or his solicitor what he
proposes, usually he will suggest that the vendor makes
a statutory declaration that he has used the way for twelve
years or more and this is usually thought of as acceptable.
The same goes for position of fences etc. If you come across
the one case in a thousand where rights of way etc. are diabolically complicated, but nevertheless the house is virtually
unique, the house of your dreams and a bargain to boot,
what do you do? You go to your Reference Library and find
a tome on Conveyancing such as Emmett on Title or Gibson's
Conveyancing and thumb through the Index until you come
to the bit about what is bothering you and read up the suggested remedy as with the statutory declaration mentioned above.
You will be very unlucky if you come across such a purchase
which throws up quasi-legal defects but if you do you simply
have to make a common-sense appraisal of whether to drop
the matter or to try going forward with the purchase by letting
a lawyer have a look in Emmett and Co. to see if there is a
remedy.

It would be a surprise if you found a house that had electricity which was not connected to the mains. The owner
would probably be so proud of his generator and his indep-
endence of "those wicked power workers" that he would
show it off without being asked. If the gas supply were bottled
you could hardly miss the evidence. Nevertheless, check both.

If you have any doubt about the water supply, have a
swift look for the lid of the cast iron box which houses the
stop-tap and is usually to be found just outside the boundary

to the front garden. If you are buying out in the sticks and think the water supply may be coming to you across someone else's land, write to the local water authority and ask them. If the vendor or his solicitor had anything about them there should be such a letter in existence from the previous transaction when he bought. Even if there is, it will still be worth while to write, quoting the letter and asking if things remain the same.

Drains can be a bit of a stinker. All your life you have simply pulled the string or pushed the plug, and what had to go has gone, and you never had to give a second thought as to where it was going or how it could possibly get there. The thought that it would answer back and refuse to go was too awful to contemplate. If you are buying in a built-up area you can be pretty sure it goes into the main drain, where it goes after that we don't worry our heads.

If a house is not connected with the main sewer, it will almost certainly drain into a septic tank, and if it does, the owner, every two or three years, depending on the size of his family, will need to have it emptied. This is no problem. Everything functions as though one had a mains drainage, but when the tank is emptied, by hydraulics into a tanker, there is a bill to pay. When the water authorities were allowed to send their bills separately from the council rate accounts, they divided the bill between water and sewerage charges. At which the septic tank owners said "Oh, no!" (not being connected to the main sewer) and so the water authorities reduced their bills to these people substantially. All of which little excursion into recent history is to tell you that the water authority bill, unless it has a specific charge for "sewerage", will tell you that you do not have connection to the main sewer, and if you are presently living in a house with a septic tank and are paying full rate for sewerage, you should get a letter off to the water authority to have the bill adjusted and to get a rebate for previous years overpaid, before reading another word.

More difficult to establish is whether you drain through anyone else's land or vice-versa. The cases where this is likely

is where a house has been built in the garden of another
house. It could become really important if you wanted to
build an extension or garage. So have a look round at the manholes, you might learn something, but as manholes have sometimes been covered over, this inspection may not be sufficient.
If you intend spending a lot of money on your extension or
garage, get your builder in to have a poke around, — if there
is bad news, he will delight in giving it you. If it is not all that
important but you like belt and braces, look in the yellow
pages for a firm that specialises in sniffing around the drains
and get a quote.

The Enquiries before Contract form tells you that no
building requiring planning permission has been carried out in
the last four years. Does that square with what you find on
inspection? Extensions or garages of less than 1750 cubic feet
don't require permission. But they still have to get, and be
built in accordance with building regulation approval, which
is a different thing from planning approval. If your vendor
gives a categorical answer "No" or even (if he has lived in
the house for more than four years) the time honoured "not
as far as I am aware", you may think that sufficient. A solicit-
or would, unless someone, like his client, alerted him otherwise.

Vendors: Receive any supplementary questions and answer
them as best you can.

Purchasers: Receive answers to supplementary questions and
decide whether to settle for what you are being offered.
If you are satisfied you can now involve yourself in the expense
of sending off a few forms together with their appropriate
fees.

Form of application for a search "Bankruptcy Only" K16
is sent to Land Charges, Plymouth. Enter your name and
address and the name of your spouse if buying in joint names,
affix 50p in stamps for each name to be searched, and post off.*
Your building society will eventually ask for the reply you
will receive. Enquiries of District Councils (CON 29A), or if
your purchase is in a London Borough Council or Corporation

*Not more than a fortnight before completion. Don't forget to enter the vendors' names too.

of London area, CON 29D LONDON form together with Search of Local Land Charges LLC1 can be sent winging on their way to the local council about the same time as you sent Enquiries Before Contract Form to Skinner, but if you take my advice you will take them round to the council offices yourself and do a *real* search around for yourself while you are there. Solicitors post these two forms. But I suggest you take them to the council offices, hand them in and ask if you can have a look at the development map and the planning applications approved and pending. Don't attempt to use the jargon. Keep it simple. If my experience is anything to go by you will get two surprises. Firstly, how much help you get if you start the service by smiling and saying to the official "I wonder if you can help me" and secondly, the amount of information you can so easily pick up, that you won't if you simply rely on the forms.

Every Local Authority has a town development map. Every good Estate Agent will have a copy. The map is divided up and each division is coloured. Some are even coloured and hatched. How a division is categorised tells you what the council intend for it. If the area is coloured say a dirty brown with black dots, it could mean that the area is intended for obnoxious industries. If anyone owns a house in that area and he wants planning permission to convert it to a bone and bladder boiling factory he might get it. A nicely coloured pink area might mean an area primarily intended for resid-ential use, and if you send off your forms of local search, those are the kind of answers you will receive. This is to say you would learn: it is an area intended for say, obnoxious indust-ries, green belt, inner ring road or residential — and that is all.

If you want to know if anyone is even thinking about doing something nasty at the bottom of the garden — ask. Particularly if you are buying property bordered by a peace-ful plot of land containing succulent fruit and veg. and even better where beyond the prospective patch there are open fields. What a lovely view. What a set up for anger and frust-ration if you simply send off the forms in the usual manner and wait for what the gods send. You could finish up looking at a brick wall and someone else's line full of washing where you thought you had a view over the undulating countryside. As soon as you saw the builders coming you would be off to your legal advisers asking what you could do about it and why you had not been told what to expect. You will now find that in addition to facing a brick wall you are banging your head on one and paying legal fees for the privilege of doing it. That's when it will be borne in on you that in spite of all your 'O' levels, 'A' levels, degrees and diplomas you are a twit. You bought land (with a house on it) in an area designated residential and you are now surprised when a house builder gets busy with the bricks and mortar creating residences in the area. My dear Sir, this isn't a question for a lawyer, it's plain common sense and a problem of understanding the English language!

What can you do to save yourself from twittery? When you go to the local council offices ask to see the list of planning permissions granted in the area over the last 7 years or so. (The spread of years is important — people often sit on development permission for years but councils give the permission subject to time limits which vary — ask). Then be really cute and ask for the list of planning applications pending! There's many a twit, who let a solicitor buy a house for him in the firm assurance that there was no planning permission for say, a road widening, only to see and hear the bulldozers arrive a year or two later. If he'd looked at the pendings he would have known that arguments about the road had been going on for years. A little tip: if a road is more pot-holed than usual it could be a sign that the council have plans for the area — obviously they will not be spending the rate-payer's money on doing up the areas that are due for redevelopment of one kind or another in the near future.

The official will tell you when to expect the LLC1 and CON 29 to be returned to you. When they do arrive have a look through for anything unusual. So unusual is it for anything unusual to appear, the authorities have duplicated replies ready. Even so, duplicated or not, you want the job doing properly, otherwise you wouldn't be doing it yourself, so you will scrutinize each answer. If you find anything you don't understand ring up the local official and ask.

There is very little to fill in on the two forms you take to the Council Offices. Both CON29A & CON29D (LONDON) forms are in two parts. You require Part I answering and it will cost you a £5.75p fee to have that done for you and you will learn from the replies you receive about such things as whether the road fronting the property is maintained at the public expense, whether the council are about to grab any land within 50 yards of your boundary in order to lay new roads, and whether they or the appropriate Secretary of State intends constructing a road, underpass, overpass, flyover or elevated road within 200 yards of the property. (The form does not ask about **201** *yards plus*, that is why D.I.Y. conveyancers come off best, because they have a chat with the officials). If you are thinking about buying a house that only has septic tank drainage and for some reason you would prefer to drain into the council drains it is this form which will elicit such information for you in Part I for your £5.75p.

Part II of CON29A or CON29D (LONDON) won't get answered by the Council unless you specifically asked them to do so. Have a look down the thirteen questions and see if you think any of them might have a bearing on the house you are interested in buying. It will cost you an extra 45p for each of the questions in part II that you initial as an indication to the officials that you require that particular question answering. The kind of things you can learn from initialling a question range from "Has the Council authorised the service of a building preservation notice?" to "Has the Council or the Secretary of State authorised the making of an order for the compulsory acquisition of the property?"

The Requisition for a Search of the local land charges register form LLC1 is even easier to complete. It has to be sent in duplicate and as it constitutes only one sheet and the form comes to you with a copy, all you have to do is insert a carbon, tick that you require all the register searching, put the address of your intended purchase and your own name and address in, pay £1.25p and that is it.*

*Local Authority fees tend to change. The fees are printed on the forms which also change from time to time.

You, the **Purchaser** can now turn your attention to the draft contract. It has to be read through and a decision made as to whether the terms are acceptable or not. It is not a take-it-or-leave-it situation — that is why it is a *draft* contract. If there is anything about which you are not clear speak to the vendor, his solicitor, or both, and get one or the other to explain (not explain away with excuses such as "it's usual") until you understand. If there is anything with which you cannot agree strike it out. Here are nine points you should watch out for when perusing the *draft* contract.

1. Has the solicitor written in all the items which the vendor said he was including in the price agreed?

2. Is the amount of deposit stated correctly? If you are getting a 95% mortgage you don't want to be bound to paying a 10% deposit. In any case if because your purchase is dependent on the sale of your present abode you might have difficulty finding a full deposit without recourse to a bridging loan, see how far you can bargain the amount of deposit down.

3. Check to whom and under what conditions the deposit is to be paid, i.e., you should insist that whosoever receives the deposit does so as stakeholder, because a stakeholder cannot part with the money unless he has been satisfied that completion has taken place. You may have paid a 'holding deposit' to an agent, or even the whole amount of the deposit, if so, the clause about the deposit should take care of that situation.*

4. There should be a clause stating the capacity in which the vendor sells. If such a clause does not appear in the draft contract, ask for one to be inserted. The usual capacity is "beneficial owner", and from a purchaser's point of view this is the best because it implies assurances such as that the vendor is the owner of the house and has the right to sell it. If he sells it by power of attorney, you are

---

*Lately some solicitors are trying to slip in a clause saying that the vendor is authorised to use your deposit monies as a deposit on his proposed purchase. Don't allow it. You never know where your money could finish up in a chain.

entitled to a copy of the power; if as executor or administrator, probate or letters of administration with Will annexed out of Principal Registry or District Probate Registry is sufficient proof of a person's death (vendors will find in Chapter 15 how to obtain those documents). In the rare case of a lender selling after a borrower's default you will be pleased to hear that you do not concern yourself with whether the "mortgagee (one who lent) in possession" is properly exercising his rights under the mortgage. But do not worry too much, 99% of vendors are beneficial owners and if yours isn't, ask their solicitor either to make them into one, or give you real evidence that they have the right to sell.

5. **Here** is a nice easy one for you: check that the address and/or description of the property to be sold is correct. There should also be a plan attached to the contract — check the land with it.

6. If you were told that you are buying a freehold, check that it says so in the description.

7. If your vendor agreed to include items such as carpets in the sale price, they should be in the contract, but if the price you are paying is just over the level at which stamp duty becomes payable, or at a level where a higher rate is demanded, fix a price for the item (£x) and ask that the clause has added to it "and £x of the purchase price shall be apportioned to these items". This will have the effect of bringing the figure on which you will pay stamp duty to the actual price you are paying for the land, bricks and mortar. On the other hand take account of how this will affect your mortgage. Building Societies don't lend on furnishings so say their maximum advance is 90% and you are buying at £24,000 — your top mortgage is £21,600, so if there is £2,000 worth of carpets etc. included in the

purchase price the highest the building society surveyor can value the house at is £22,000 and the
maximum advance is £19,800 so your deposit now
becomes £4,200 instead of the number you first
thought of. The rest of the sums on which your decision rests I leave to your honesty and ingenuity.

8. Look at the rate of interest typed into the contract.
This is usually 2% above bank base rate. You will
be expected to pay interest at that rate if you delay
completion beyond the date which eventually gets
inserted in the contract. The most likely reason for
you getting caught with having to pay this type
of interest will be if your purchase monies are dependent on the sale monies from your present house,
and you can't make your purchaser complete simultaneously with your own purchase. So make sure
the date in your purchase contract is the same as
in your sale contract, and have your purchaser
tied to 2% above bank base rate also, then you have
a source from which to collect any penalty money.

9. Restrictive covenants clause. With the draft contract Skinner should send you a copy of all the restrictive covenants. There is not much you can do
about them, but you certainly want to know everything there is to know about them, because you buy
property, warts and all, and once you are the owner,
you will be responsible for seeing that the covenants
(if any) are adhered to. You can also ask to be
assured that the previous owners have kept to the
covenants. For instance, if there is a covenant that
only a certain type of house should be built on the
plot and plans should have been approved and
agreed by some previous owner, ask to see the app-
rovals.

If there is anything in the contract you feel needs to be
amended, do so and send it back to the vendor for his approval.

Vendors: If you are selling to some smart alec who has read the above, send what he asks for if you have it, if not, and you can say so truthfully, write back "I do not have in the deeds what you ask for, I have never received any notice of any breach of covenant". Otherwise, if you can, simply accept the alterations and let the purchaser know that you do.

Purchaser: A solicitor would get nothing better out of a vendor's solicitor and after all, it makes sense, because if a person who could complain hasn't, the longer it goes on, the less likelihood there is of a court giving an order that the breach be repaired. Faced with a demand that a pitched roof which was built ten years ago be altered to a flat roof, simply because it says only flat roofs in a covenant entered into twenty years ago, where is the judge who would give judgement against the owner? If no objection was raised either at the time the breach occurred or soon after, the covenant in question would no doubt be held to have been waived and the longer the breach has gone without objection the more certain you can be in assuming that it has been waived.

However, if you really have reason to believe that there has been a recent breach of covenant, then try to insure against a claim. If the insurance company with all its millions won't play, you need either an appropriate reduction in the price, strong gambler's nerves, or to start looking at other properties. You will be very unlucky if this happens to you. When agreement has been reached on the draft contract, you can put it to one side and give your attention to the replies you will have received to your enquiries of the district council.

CON 29: "Enquiries of District Councils" usually comes back with a printed list of answers. In 999 cases out of 1,000 it will confirm that the road is made up, taken over and maintained at public expense; that there are no road widening proposals, and no proposals to build a new road within 200 yards of the property. If you had been afraid lest the council had an army of workmen at the ready, itching to get on with demolishing a garage or extension which had previously been built infringing building regulations and planning permission the replies will either confirm your suspicions or put your mind at rest.

If it turns out that the road is about to be made up, you will want to know what the cost is likely to be and how much the vendor is prepared to knock off the price to meet it. If the property is about to be pulled down for slum clearance or the infringement of building regulations your course of action is obvious.

Having called at the council office you will have put flesh on the bones of the more-or-less standard answers on the form. You will have found out if there is to be a motorway within 201 yards or whether there is any redevelopment scheme in the offing that could affect the property, being either a whole shopping precinct, or an application to convert the quaint little antique shop on the corner into a fish and chip shop. In the unlikely event of you getting a reply which you do not understand, either call in on the council or give them a ring.

Form LLC1 will no doubt drop through your letter-box at about the same time. The council will either certify that "the search requested reveals no subsisting registrations" or "the search reveals the registrations described in the schedules hereto......" If there are any schedules attached they are likely to refer to smoke control and planning controls that have long since been dealt with. The search might show that an improvement grant was agreed. That does not mean to say the grant was taken up, but you will want to know from the vendor if it was and if so whether any part of it has to be repaid on a sale taking place. If there is any verbiage that you don't understand in the replies to your searches and you think it could affect you, ring up the council and ask — council officials are invariably helpful to the D.I.Y. conveyancer.

You are now almost in a position to send off your signed part of the contract either in the form it was originally drafted or as amended by agreement. There are a couple of things to be watched: 1. Arrange for the property to be insured, as from the signing of contracts it is at your risk. If between exchange and completion the house should go up in a puff of smoke the buyer has still to go forward with the purchase. I suppose this bit of property law is intended to dissuade a purchaser who has seen something cheaper and better, from trying to slide out of the contract by the simple expedient of slipping round to the property and striking a box of matches under it. So insure for the usual risks, such as fire, storm, flood, tempest, burglars, and owner's liability for damage done to atheists who can't or won't believe in Acts of God when slates drop onto their heads. In its offer of a mortgage, the Building Society may already have nominated an insurance company. Unless you have some root and branch objections to the nominees get your insurance with them; then write and let the Building Society know. 2: Check that the offer of a mortgage which you have received is a firm one. In addition, if your purchase is dependent on receiving the monies from your own sale you will realize that ideally the contracts should be signed simultaneously, but this is difficult to imagine because it entails getting all the parties together at the same time in the same place, and if everyone is taking the same precaution then all would need to be ambidextrous. The only sensible solution, therefore, if your purchase is dependent on your own sale is to make *absolutely* certain that you have received your sale contract signed by your purchaser and that any conditional clauses can and will be met, before you sign up to buy.

So here is your check list on the eve of exchange of contracts.

1. Draft contract has been agreed and one of your copies has been returned unsigned to vendor.

2. Satisfactory replies have been received to your Enquiries before Contract Form CON29 (Long).

3. You are satisfied with the replies you received to the forms you sent to the Council CON29 and LLC1 and what you learned on your fact finding tour.

4. If the Office Copies revealed anything such as a caution or a Matrimonial Home charge the vendor

has already given you satisfactory written assurances that he can obtain a release from the cautioner.

5. You have got a firm offer of a mortgage.

6. You have insurance.

7. If it applies, you have your own sale tied up.*

8. You have checked that everyone over the age of 18 who lives in the house is prepared to move whether their names appear on the register or not.

All this might seem work for a detail maniac but you've heard about the "thousand things that can go wrong" in in housing transactions. I've never seen a detailed list but the things that do go wrong in real life I have tried to alert you to so that they won't go wrong for you.

Hopefully you have enough money stashed away under the piano lid to pay the deposit and have pushed the amount required down to your level as recommended earlier.

So here goes! Insert the agreed date for completion. This is usually one month hence, so if you feel there is still a lot of reading left in this chapter also remember there is one month to do it in. There is no reason why it shouldn't be earlier than the usual month if it will save either party money to be paid on bridging loans. Sign the contract and send it off to Mr. Skinner together with the balance of the agreed deposit.

Vendor: we have not forgotten you! The astute reader will have realized by now how little a vendor has to know or do in order to be his own conveyancer. However, you must rouse yourself, at this point, to receive the signed contract from the purchaser. Check that the contract he has signed is identical to the one you agreed to and have a word with the stakeholder to make sure the balance of the deposit has been paid.

Even if your purchaser is getting 100% mortgage, I think you should still insist on a deposit. After all, if he is such a good risk that the lender doesn't require him to have a

*If a deposit cheque bounces the contract is automatically washed out.

stake in the house he should have no difficulty in raising a bank loan for 5% of the purchase price. If you don't get a deposit your contract is shaky. As pointed out before there is a difference between having rights and asserting them; you really cannot get blood out of a stone and possession really is nine points of the law. Sign your copy of the contract and send it to the purchaser.

Contracts are now said to be exchanged. The deal is now binding and neither side can back out without penalty. If you have a mortgage on the property write to your building society telling them that contracts have been exchanged. Give them the venue for completion if this has been determined and ask them how much will be required to pay off your mortgage on the completion date. Also ask for the daily rate that will be charged in the unlikely event of completion being delayed. Also write to your Insurance Company asking for a rebate on the unexpired portion of the last annual premium you paid.

Purchaser: receive vendor's part of the contract and check details. Pay particular attention that both parties have signed if it is owned by man and wife. While all this has been going on you have been dealing with the solicitor for the building society. Every building society has what it calls a roll of solicitors who act for it in the completion of mortgage advances. The building society has sent a surveyor to the property to see if it is a good enough security for the money they are lending to you and they also need a solicitor to say whether you are getting good title to the property, and to handle the signing of the mortgage deed and the crucial finale of handing over the money.

I have never heard of a solicitor who applied to have his name put on the roll of a building society being refused, so most solicitors are on the rolls of most building societies, and it is a simple matter for them so to be if they wish it. So when a purchaser gets a mortgage, what do you know, the solicitor acting for him in his purchase, also gets instructions to act for the building society. It makes sense by saving too many solicitors trailing round to too many other solicitors' offices to complete a sale. Just because you are acting for yourself, it doesn't mean to say that you can't try to take advantage of the system. Your mortgage application form will ask for the name of the solicitor acting for you and you will reply "self". So have a word with the manager at your building society branch when you take the application form in and mention who is acting for your vendor. With any luck the same solicitor will be appointed to act for the building society.

When you receive your offer of mortgage, the society will inform you who will be acting for them, and of course you will have to pay for that service.* Their solicitor will write asking you to produce a number of documents. As the information contained in the papers they request could in the future be quite useful to the do-it-yourself conveyancer I suggest you photo-copy them, because building societies usually keep the lot. This is what they require:

> Enquiries before contract and vendor's solicitor's replies.
> Local Authority search forms and replies.
> Vendor's part of the original contract.
> Land Registry Office Copies.
> Authority to inspect register.
> Copy of transfer.

You will have noticed two new items in the above list. Neither need cause you any trouble. You ask the vendor's solicitor to produce the authority to inspect the register if he hasn't with the foresight our Mr. Bold had, furnished you with two already, one for yourself and one for the building society solicitor. The other item is the transfer, the very form which does the trick of getting your vendor's name off the Land Register and putting yours on. The transfer form is No. 19 and you will remember meeting it on the very first page of this chapter, and now you come face to face with it you will find that, though of supreme importance, it is the easiest of the lot. (If you are buying on a new estate you will require Form 20 (transfer of part). The draft is usually provided by the developer because he wants to put in a swathe of conditions that were not in the conveyance of the land to him.)

*See page 177

After exchange of contracts you are expected to send a draft of the transfer form to the vendor's solicitor. Fill in the title number, which by now you will almost have memorised, the address of the property you are buying, leave a blank for the completion date, put in the price you have dragged the vendor down to, then put in the name and present address of the vendor and finish the labour by inserting your own name and new address.

If you are married or buying jointly with someone else decide what is to happen when one of you dies. Husbands and wives nearly always used to buy as joint tenants, so that the survivor escaped paying death duties on half the probate valuation of the house. With the coming of Capital Transfer Tax this is no longer a problem as capital transfer tax does not have to be paid on what one spouse leaves to another. However, it all costs the same whether the house is registered in one name or two. So if you are buying jointly put both your names. If two names are not those of spouses, the house can still be owned so that survivor takes all or so that the dead partner's share goes into his estate. In either case the Registrar has to be informed and we will deal with how later — for the moment if you want the ownership to be in joint names simply put the two names on the form.*

Finally complete the certificate of value which the revenue man requires — he doesn't trust the property-owning classes. If you can manage to buy a house for £20,000† or less you have no stamp duty to pay. Agree to pay the vendor an extra £1 if he will leave the cat-flap and with a purchase price of £20,001 you will have to pay $\frac{1}{2}$% stamp duty (£100). Being a free born Englishman the revenue man expects you to get up to every trick in the book in order to side-skip paying your money over to him. Unless you sign otherwise, he suspects you of trying to buy the house in bits. £5,000 for the billiard room, £5,000 each for each of the bathrooms and £2,000 each for each of the bedrooms and so on, all done in separate transactions. So the revenue insist that you certify that "the transfer hereby effected does not form part of a larger transaction or series of transactions in respect of which

*See also p. 138
†1983: £25,000

the amount or value or aggregate amount or value of the consideration exceeds £......".

If the purchase price is £20,000* or less that is the figure you put in. If it is more than £35,000 you cross out the clause because you become a fully paid up member and pay the full rate of 2% on the whole amount. That is to say, if you buy at £40,000 you pay stamp duty of £800. The rates are (1980) as follows: £20,000 or less — nil. From £20,001 to £25,000 — stamp duty is one half per cent. £25,001 to £30,000 — one per cent and £30,001 to £35,000 one and one half per cent. After that it is 2%.†

Vendor: receive the draft transfer and check it. If you do not receive a draft do not worry. There is so little that is open to debate about what can, should or shouldn't go in that people are, nowadays, tending to dispense with the draft procedure, and I suppose the little ritual will die the death within the next fifty years or so. After all it is only 55 years since transfers took over from conveyances in London — you can't expect people to change overnight. Check draft for clerical errors and approve.

Purchaser: *Your conveyancing doesn't have to be done overnight.* If from reading the instructions so far it seems to you that there are a lot of fiddling little things to do, bear in mind three things. In the first place they are mainly technical and not legal, secondly, even after contracts are exchanged you will have at least a month to do it all in, and lastly, but fruitiest of the lot — a number of people's hopes are riding on your buying the house and it is surprising how helpful others can be when they *need* to be.

Send off two Requisitions on Title Forms Con 28B. This form asks questions about the date for completion and what money will be required i.e. a completion statement. It also asks the vendor to produce receipts for outgoings and is mainly referring to rates. If the Enquiries before Contract Form were completed again now, it asks, would the replies be as they were hitherto. Question four concerns mortgages. It starts strongly with "all subsisting mortgages must be discharged on or before

*1983: £25,000
†March 1982 budget added £5,000 to all the prices in this paragraph.

completion" but then weakens and goes on to ask what form of undertaking to hand over receipts is proposed. Now an undertaking to hand over the discharge of a building society mortgage is always acceptable — but not so for any other mortgagee, particularly one with "Ltd." after its name. So if on the charge register of the office copies you received, there was a charge (charge means mortgage) to a finance company — indeed to anybody other than a building society, write in the space provided for additional questions: "Form 53(co) (53 if an individual lender) to be handed over on completion together with charge certificate duly sealed and signed".

While you are about it you might as well write in that the vendor's solicitor will provide any information and documents you will require in order to register your ownership. You never know what the registrar might ask for and a solicitor might, just for fun, retain papers or information you are going to need. A solicitor won't play silly-billies with a brother building society solicitor who will be doing the registering if you are taking a mortgage, but it could be very important to get agreement to the above point if you are a cash buyer and come up against the kind of solicitor who likes practical jokes and even thinks that the conundrums in Christmas crackers are excruciatingly funny.* Also use the space at the end of the form into which you can feed any additional questions that your Building Society may ask in response to the documents you will have sent them. Their response will also almost certainly include three other things:

1. The printed mortgage form for you to sign in front of a witness. Have a scan through the mortgage form (legal charge) but don't invite a headache. It is a take-it-or-leave-it situation — no variations are allowed. If you have to sign forms which lay down, among other things, that if you do not keep the gutters clear they can come with workmen, remedy the situation and send you the bill and that makes them happy, it would be school marming to deny them. Sometimes a society's form provides that

*Also see p.124

the witness be a solicitor and that is usually alright but as you are not using a solicitor arrange one of two things with such a society: either to sign on completion in front of their solicitor or for them to waive the point. It isn't a legal requirement, being neither oath nor statutory declaration.

2. An account made up of the fees you have to pay their solicitor, plus stamp duties. The total will be deducted from the cheque produced on completion day.

3. A sheet of requisitions (questions) about your purchase. Societies don't have a standard form, but you will find that the questions cover more or less the same ground as you did to the vendor's solicitor with your enquiries before contract. Copy off the answers you were given and if there are any you haven't already got the answers to, get onto the vendor's solicitor right away and get the answers back to the society as quickly as possible in case they raise supplementaries, as you can do without being harassed by their questions right up to completion day.

    This form will also ask you if you intend to live in the house and to confirm that the whole of the difference between the mortgage advance and the purchase money is being found out of your own resources and without recourse to any other form of borrowing. The building society might also enclose a list of any further documents they require on completion. If they don't, ask them to let you have such a list as soon as possible.

Vendor: receive Requisition on Title (CON28B). If your purchaser's solicitor is asking for things you simply do not have, say so. Remember, when you bought you no doubt paid a highly trained solicitor to check out that you were getting good title so if he was satisfied on your behalf then your purchaser's solicitor should be happy with what his brother in the law did.

Make up a completion statement as requested by showing purchase price minus deposit paid plus anything you require to re-imburse you for water rates paid in advance. Don't worry about the general rates because they are levied on the occupier, simply let the Local Authority know the date you are moving out and if you have managed to pay for rates you haven't used they will re-imburse you. The Water Authorities vary in the way they run their show, so divine their system, and show in your completion statement how much Mr. Feather will have to pay in order to re-imburse you for the amount you have paid in advance.

Purchaser: receive replies to Requisitions on Title Form CON 28B and completion statement. If you are buying without a mortgage you can skip the next bit until we come to Form 94A. About this time you should be in possession of the list of documents your Building Society will require on completion. They will always require a minimum of:

1. Vendor's land certificate (or charge certificate if the house is mortgaged).

2. Vendor's building society solicitor's undertaking to send a Land Registry form discharging vendor's mortgage.

3. Transfer Form 19* signed by vendor.

These three forms you will, of course, receive from Mr. Skinner on completion.

The rest of the documents your Building Society will ask you to produce are:-

4. Mortgage form (Legal Charge) signed by you.

5. L.A.451 sometimes referred to as P.D. form† (particulars delivered form) obtainable from Inland Revenue stamp offices — There are stamp offices at London, Birmingham, Bristol, Cardiff, Leeds, Liverpool, Manchester, Newcastle, Nottingham and Sheffield.

*Form 20 or 43 if buying from a builder
† p.140 for completion instructions

You have to complete one of these whether stamp duty is payable or not. It's the job you will be used to by now of filling in names and addresses. The only two bits of jargon you will come on will be firstly "Description of Instrument", and the answer is Transfer, and the second is "Estate or interest transferred", the answer to which is the address of the house you are buying.

6. The reply you received to the form K16 which you sent to Land Charges Registry.

7. Form 94A Application by Purchaser for Official Search. Again a name-and-address job, plus enter date of issue of office copy. An important form this, which was mentioned in Chapter 9 "The Registers" so we won't labour it again. Suffice to say that you are enquiring of the registry whether anyone has registered any dealings in the land since the date the office copies were made for you.

There is no fee to pay for this service but you must enclose the written authority of the registered proprietor, or his solicitor, to inspect the register. Don't send this form off until about ten days before the date agreed for completion for, as you will see it gives you protection (Priority Expires box) for 16 working days (3 weeks plus 1 day) in which to complete and register your deal. Though this is a building society requirement you should use this form even if you are not taking a mortgage. If you are buying from a landlord who has other properties registered under the same title No. or a builder who is developing an area of land, use Form 94B, Search of Part. The Registry need to know which part and it is up to the vendor to provide you with sufficient identification, (plans, plot No. etc.) to satisfy the Registrar.*

8. Form A4. Application for Registration of Dealings in Registered Titles. One point to which you need give a little thought is Question 4 which requires a

*Protection given is now 30 days.

YES or NO answer. If two persons are buying they must decide whether they want survivor to take all — if so the answer is YES.

You might not be absolutely certain exactly which forms and documents will be "lodged herewith" as Panel 1 requires. Don't worry, you can safely rely on the Building Society and Skinner to help you out on completion day, because you are not the only party to this deal and matters have gone so far by now, that in 999 cases out of 1,000 your vendor is just as anxious to see the colour of your money as you are to see that of the man who is buying your present abode. So you have them. And as Richard Nixon said, "When you have them by the balls, their hearts and minds are sure to follow!"

Vendor. Sign the transfer form and get your spouse to sign beside you if the house is in joint names. If you have no mortgage to pay off choose your spot for completion. If you have a mortgage then as the Charge Certificate and the rest of the papers will have been sent to the building society's solicitor, you will have to use his office. The building society solicitor doesn't have much to do, but nevertheless he charges the building society and they in turn charge you by adding his fees onto the outstanding balance of your account with them. His job is to collect and give a receipt for the money and hand over the Charge Certificate to you. Why this bit of a job cannot be done by building societies' local managers I cannot understand, and as do-it-yourself conveyancing proliferates, as it surely will, I will be surprised if they do not take over the slight functions which solicitors now perform and charge so heavily for.* Bank managers cope with loans secured on property and I am sure that every single building society manager I have ever met had as much about him as any bank manager who is entrusted with this kind of work.

Let your purchaser know the venue and exact time. Also inform him that you will require the balance of the purchase

*Since writing these prophetic words the slow takeover has begun. Hallelujah! J.B.

price in the form of a banker's draft, which has the advantage over a cheque, that it cannot be stopped and it will not bounce.

If you have a mortgage to pay off ask for the money to be split into two drafts and give the figures i.e. one draft made out to your building society for the amount required to pay off your mortgage and the balance for yourself, or if such is the case, made out to the vendor (or his solicitor) of the house you are buying.* You can work out the permutations for yourself if more than two drafts would be useful to you. The important thing is to *make sure all the balance comes by bankers draft or cash.*

Purchaser. Receive the completion statement and request about how the money is to be split. If you don't receive them seven days before completion gee the other side up — you will soon have plenty of problems coping with crockery and curtain runners, without having uninvited last minute jobs to do on the financial side.

You have no doubt bought and sold motor cars in the past. Collecting the money on one, paying out on another; paying off the H.P. on one and obtaining H.P. on another, are all very fiddly, all on the surface very complicated. Housing transactions are much the same, the big difference being that when the proceeds from the sale of one car is being used to purchase another, both cars can be at the scene of completion. Unless you are moving next door or across the street this is not possible with housing transactions. So look at the purchase at this stage as being of the title deeds (the Land or Charge Certificate and the Transfer Form) which represent the house. Anyway, approach the financial side of completion of your purchase as you did swapping cars and you won't go far wrong.

Vendor. If you have a mortgage and completion is not to take place at the purchaser's solicitor's office ring him up and remind him what day it is. Clutching signed Form 19, the Land Certificate (if your house is paid for) and the keys to your house, hie you to the venue for completion at the appointed hour. You are selling the keys and the title deeds.

*Lender might now ask you for a form 53 (Co.). If so, you will need lender's full name as shown at entry 6 of our example on p.73.

When you have handed them over that is that. So make sure you get the last penny in real money before parting. The purchaser's solicitor will have a quick look at Form 19 to make sure the bits that are filled in are the same as you showed in your draft. If you have a mortgage to pay off he will hand the society's solicitor the draft he requires to redeem your mortgage, and hand you a draft for the balance made out as you requested. The deposit which was paid to the stakeholder is now due to you so the purchaser's solicitor will hand you an authority to collect it from the stakeholder.

Have a root round among the papers you got when you bought the house. If you got a copy of your mortgage form (Charge, Legal Charge), take it along with you because, more than likely, it will have a form of receipt. When the Building Society solicitor gets his bank draft you can ask him to complete the receipt. If you can't find aforementioned Charge ask for a receipt to say you've paid it off. It's not vital, but you might as well be on the absolutely safe side. Don't worry about satisfying the purchaser that your mortgage is paid off as your Building Society Solicitor will do that. So having got the balance of the purchase price and the letter releasing the deposit hand over the signed transfer and Land Certificate if applicable, and the keys and go on your way rejoicing. *You've sold your house.*

Purchaser. Rejoice that we are now coming to the last round up.

Gather together the documents that your Building Society solicitor said he would require to be handed over on completion (see page 108). Get your bank draft for the balance of the purchase price and if the vendor's solicitor is not holding the deposit write a letter authorising the stakeholder to release the deposit to the vendor or his solicitor.

Arrange with the vendor or his agent for the keys to be available to you or your representative (you can't be in two places at once) for a swift inspection to make sure that everything that was to be left in is still there and everyone who was to move out has gone; that you are truly getting vacant possession on completion. If anyone is still there *do not complete*, no matter what fanciful explanations or excuses are tried on you. Such a case is but one in a million, but who wants to be a statistic? Incidentally, very few and very, very far between are the solicitors who would go to the trouble of a last-minute inspection on your behalf. Greater in number and nearer together are those who might mention to you that it would not be a bad idea, and if you can manage it old boy, etc. etc. This final inspection is done in order to avoid the greatest calamity of all that can possibly befall the purchaser of a house intended for his own and immediate occupation. So whether employing a solicitor or doing your own conveyance **make sure you are getting vacant possession.**

If you did not manage to persuade your building society to appoint your vendor's solicitor to act for them when you got your mortgage you will find whoever was appointed is present at the completion appointment and you will hand over to him the documents he has asked for. You will be on foreign territory but politely refuse to be overawed. The other parties might well not be solicitors, but clerks, trying not to show *their* awe of a man such as you, who can afford to buy such a swish residence and meet the colossal regular outgoings that everybody knows go with such ownership.

The vendor's solicitor then hands to you the transfer (Form 19) and either the Land Certificate (if vendor did not have a mortgage) or Charge Certificate (if he did). You can differentiate between the two by a mere glance at the very large print on the covers. Now check that the Land or Charge Certificate is the same as the office copies you received at the outset and that the transfer (Form 19) has the same infilling as the draft you prepared and had approved and that the parties to the sale have signed and had their signatures witnessed. Hand the Land or Charge Certificate and the transfer to your Building Society solicitor together with your legal charge to them if you are taking a mortgage — if not pop them in your shopping bag.

If you are not taking a mortgage you will require an undertaking from the vendor's building society solicitor that he will produce within 14 days after completion a form 53 discharging the vendor's mortgage. If you are taking a mortgage then the vendor's building society solicitor will give the form 53 directly to the solicitor acting for your building society.

You now produce your banker's draft for any balance needed to make up the difference between the purchase price and the mortgage monies which the building society solicitor now hands over. You also give over the letter releasing the deposit and then receive the keys at best or a letter to the key holder. **The job is done. You've got yourself a new house!**

During the last few pages references to yourself, your building society solicitor, the vendor's solicitor, his building society solicitor and, where you are selling, at the same time, your purchaser's solicitor and his building society solicitor, not to mention the building society solicitor for your own sale if you are changing societies, could lead you to think that for completion day you might have to book St. Pancras Town Hall or put up a marquee (light refreshments to be served) in the garden. NOT SO. Solicitors are capable of wearing many hats at the same time and you'll no doubt finish up with only one if you're a first time buyer, or two if you are involved in a chain.

About three months after completion you can send off a form A44 and 75p to the Land Registry for one set of 'Registry Entries' and within a fortnight you will receive a set of office copies showing yourself as the proprietor.

If you are buying without a mortgage there are a couple of little things for you to do which, had you been taking a mortgage, the Building Society solicitor would have done for you.

1. The transfer has to be stamped at an Inland Revenue Stamp office, or a head post office. Even if you are buying (1980) for £20,000 and there is no duty to pay you still need it stamping P.D. (particulars delivered). Send the transfer with LA451 and cheque if necessary to stamp office.

2. Register your ownership Form A4 "Application for Registration of Dealings with the WHOLE of the

Land comprised in one or more registered titles."
Complete the A4, parcel it up with the Land Certificate (or Charge Certificate) together with Form
53 which your vendor's building society has produced in accordance with their undertaking) the
transfer form 19 and your green search form 94A.
Include the fee which you ascertain by ringing Land
Registry Enquiries Dept. You keep an eye on the
date protection ends and try to get the Form 53 in
time, but if you can't, send what you have got and
apply for an extension.

If you are buying a house from say a landlord who owns
the whole block or a builder who has developed an area of
land, your vendor will have his title to what is now being split
up into bits registered as a whole under one title number, so
the procedure is just that little bit different. Instead of A4
Dealings with WHOLE you will use Form A5 Dealings with
Part. The Land Registry will, of course, want to know which
part and it is up to the vendor to provide you with sufficient
identification material (i.e. plans, with plot or house No.) to
satisfy the Registrar, which you will already have obtained
when sending in your form for "search of part", as instructed
earlier.

In this Chapter and the ones on Contract, Mortgages and
Registered Land I have covered the typical and some not very
typical situations that can arise. If you come across anything
else that does not yield to common sense, and the Land Registry
enquiries department is not able or empowered to help you
with, go to your nearest reference library or university library,
walk boldly up to the nearest assistant and ask to be shown
where to find a few useful books such as Wontner's Guide to
Land Registry Practice, Emmott on Title, or Gibson's Conveyancing. If when you've made a search of the indices you can
find no answer to your problem, have a wash, a breath of
fresh air and try again.

From a buyer saying "I will" to completion taking
place occupies two to three calendar months, so you needn't
feel rushed.

12. Doing the Sale and Purchase of an Unregistered House

At page 86 barely a dozen lines were used to describe all that has to be done to transfer ownership of registered property in England and Wales.

What about unregistered? It is supposed to be more difficult, or so we are told. Judge for yourself.

Same scenario as page 86.

Proud owner: Here is a conveyance which is more than fifteen years old. As you see, it is signed by me and the previous owner, stamped by the Inland Revenue, and it contains the restrictive covenants saying what one can and cannot do in and around the property. Here is a photo-copy from which you can make a conveyance from me to you on stout paper (engrossing paper if you can get any) putting me in as the vendor this time and yourself as the purchaser. Alter the date and the price and I will sign it for you, give you the original and the keys in exchange for the money and off you go to get it stamped.

Honestly, that's it!

If a vendor bought less than fifteen years ago he must produce not only his own conveyance but also other deeds that make up a chain going back at least the fifteen years required for "good root of title".

A deed is an instrument in writing signed, sealed and

delivered; such an instrument of transfer of property from one person to another is called a conveyance. If you were the cautious buyer of a second-hand lawn mower, and asked the seller to prove it was his to sell, he would produce the receipt. It is the same with an unregistered house. The first part of any conveyance shows this clearly as you can see from our specimen conveyance, p. 146.

Like the lawn mower buyer, the purchaser of a house needs to be convinced that what the vendor is offering is his to sell. This is usually done by producing a copy of the conveyance which the vendor got when he bought. It will be something like our specimen. A copy of the covenants referred to will come with the draft contract. If the date on the conveyance, showing the present vendor as the purchaser, is more than 15 years old, he has proved title, because when X Lax moved, his solicitor proved to Strong's solicitor that everything was in order.

It seems to be assumed that if, within 15 years of a person taking possession of a property, no one comes along kicking up a fuss about the ownership, then everything must be in order. But what if the house has changed hands eleven times during the past 15 years? Simple enough if every transaction was a straightforward sale and purchase; you need to see eleven conveyances linked in the progression A to B; B to C; C to D; . . . K to Lax. When you are purchasing an unregistered property that has changed hands a number of times in the past 15 years, apart from wondering why it was so unloved, comfort yourself with this thought about the title: All the purchasers in the chain are likely to have employed highly trained solicitors either to check the title or to supervise their clerks' checking of it. No doubt building society solicitors will have satisfied themselves about it too. If you are taking a mortgage the lender's solicitor will be giving things the once over *at your expense* (plus VAT) and you might feel justified in relying on him. If you have any queries ask him or her. Ask nicely, you can only be refused.

It is interesting to play detective with a pile of conveyances but the important ones are the last one and the one referred to at (5) of our specimen contract for sale at p.55.

Some solicitors only send a summary of the conveyance/s which cover the previous 15 years. If your opposite number does that, add a clause to the draft contract saying that copies will be provided, and ask for them to be forwarded as soon as possible.

I have never met anyone who paid for a house and was subsequently in trouble because someone way back along a line going back to one of William the Conqueror's hangers-on hadn't the right to sell. It's the last conveyance that counts and you've met the vendor. However, if all the above and your own experience does not convince you then you are an ultra-cautious person and can obtain insurance cover from Stewart Title (UK) Ltd.

If you are such a cautious type, even if you pay a solicitor to do the conveyance of an unregistered house for you, I would still urge you to get such a policy, otherwise your mind will never be set at rest regarding your most valued possession. Be assured that the Law Society won't be a fat lot of use if it turns out that anything was wrong with a title which one of its members had thought was all right.

So it turns out that you need to check that the person named in the last link of the chain as the purchaser is the same as the one named in your contract; that the address of the house you are buying corresponds; that the plan is the same as the one sent with the draft contract, and that after the words TO HOLD it says "in fee simple" because those two words define the property as freehold (as opposed to leasehold: if it were leasehold, it would refer to the lease in the section beginning, ALL THAT).

If your vendor hasn't owned the property for 15 years or more, you will have to apply all the above checks to the conveyances which take you back over the period required.

A conveyance forms what is known as "good root of title". It is the most usual because it indicates that an investigation of the title was carried out at the time of its making, and in ninety-nine cases out of a hundred proof of ownership of the average house will be by production of a conveyance or a series of linked conveyances.

Sometimes another document is required to forge a link. Obviously, a deceased person cannot pass on ownership by making a conveyance. (If such an owner was on good terms with her/his intended heirs the conveyance will have been made earlier "by way of gift"). In such a case a devise (see glossary) is a good root and the document which forms the link between the deceased owner and the next is a copy of "probate" or "letters of administration" issued by the High Court out of the District Probate Registry which shows who was appointed to administer the deceased's estate.

When once the administrators get the property out of their hands and into those of the beneficiaries they require a "deed of release" from their responsibilities. A purchaser needs a copy of this.

A mortgage also constitutes a good root of title because presumably people don't lend money on security without first checking that the borrower owns the property.

A purchaser need not worry overmuch lest some silly solicitor, who doesn't realise the best way of getting good reports of himself in the community, fails to tip up all these documents, because in sending you the National or Law Society's Conditions of Sale contract he has bound himself to do so.

A vendor will expect to find all title documents in his deeds parcel for the same reason.

If the last five paragraphs apply to your case (and they seldom do) please read them again. After all you did not fully grasp that two plus two equalled four the first time you heard about it. At the moment you are dealing with a hypothetical case. Once you have a set of forms and documents on the table before you it will be that much easier to shuffle them about with the aid of these paragraphs. If you have any difficulty and the vendor's solicitor hasn't already sent one, ask for an "epitome of title" which is a list of the deeds that take you back to the root of title or the deed which created the covenants, or both.

In the rest of this chapter the information will be divided between that for a purchaser and that for a vendor, so that a check list, to be used in conjunction with the flow diagram, begins to appear. But don't eschew the other side's information, it's good to know what the other chap is up to, and in any case, you may well be changing roles in a few years' time.

Vendor: Your first step is to get hold of the deeds. If your house is paid for and you haven't already got the deeds at home, go to wherever they are and get them. If the property is still mortgaged, write to the Head Office of your Building Society and ask if they will send the title deeds to their branch office nearest your home, as you are selling the property, acting for yourself, and will need to make copies of relevant documents. Try your best to have the deeds sent to the Building Society office, because when you have found your purchaser it's more than possible that his solicitor could be appointed to act for the Building Society and that will save a little legwork for both you and the purchaser. Bear in mind that the title deeds are yours. They are only deposited with the lender as security for the money he has lent to you. I mention this in case someone tries to lord it over you when you go to inspect your deeds. Be bold, but as courteous as is expected of propertied people!

The bundle, though referred to as "the deeds", is made up of all sorts of papers that are and are not deeds. There will be copies of old search certificates, receipted mortgages and of course conveyances, and it is the latter with which you concern yourself at this stage. They are typed on stout paper, folded and marked on the outside front.

DATED 8th June, 1920

Mr. V. A. CATER

to

Mr. N. SCONCE

Conveyance

of all that messuage or
dwelling house known as
and situate at
14 Plevna Place, in the
County of Eden.

Wigg, Spout & Skinner
Solicitors
Blossomton

When you look at your deeds bear in mind the three things your purchaser needs to know about the property at this point: (1) That you own it (2) What, if anything, goes with it . . . rights of way etc. and (3) What can and cannot be done with it.

If you bought fifteen years or more ago your luck is in. Photocopy the conveyance to yourself, make a copy of the plan if there is one, and copy out the covenants and conditions if they are not 'recited' in your conveyance. But if, during the past fifteen years the house has changed hands a few times you will need to copy each of the conveyances covering the period that takes you back to the root of title as given at clause 5 of your contract.

But what if the house has not been built 15 years, or you bought from someone who was the first buyer after the piece of land on which it was built was split from a larger piece? In that case you can only expect to find a written summary of previous deeds on which the builder's solicitor (clerk) will have endorsed something like "examined against originals at the offices of Messrs. Skinner & Stonehart solicitors of that parish". Copy it.

You will also have to photo-copy more than the conveyance to yourself (even if you've been the owner for more than fifteen years), if the mention of restrictive covenants in your conveyance confines itself to saying that the benefits, easements and covenants are those "contained, mentioned or referred to in a conveyance dated.........between So and So and Thingumy". You root out the conveyance to Thingumy and hopefully the list is set out there of what you **HOLD/SUBJECT NEVERTHELESS** to. This is the set of capital letters which usually heralds the covenants, restrictions, etc., in a conveyance. Photo-copy the whole conveyance. Sometimes it will be easy: a straightforward conveyance to you without a covenant in sight. Sometimes you will have to beaver away at the pile.

Hopefully you will get all that is required at the first go. Even if you only think you have, *that is what matters at this stage*, because you send the lot on to your purchaser's solicitor. And if what you have sent is accepted, you move to the next step. On the other hand, if you have made some mistakes or omissions, Skinner will be only too delighted to let you know that you've missed a link in the chain, so off you go to the originals again, this time knowing precisely what you are looking for. This is only what happens between solicitors, — hence requisitions. *Easy isn't it?*

If you are not sure of your purchaser and think the sale might go off either take two copies of everything, because a solicitor might be on holiday when you request a return, or take one copy and, at this stage: (a) rely on clause 5 of your contract or (b) if there is an epitome of title, copy that and add on short notes regarding transactions since the last one mentioned on it. In your covering letter to Skinner itemize what you are sending, as a reminder for yourself and to avoid disputes later.

But for the present, concern yourself with preparing your draft contract. From the conveyance to you get the date to complete the clause beginning **WHEREBY IT IS AGREED**. If the conveyance to you is less than fifteen years old you have to rummage around to find one that is more, and put the parties and date of that into Clause 5. Clause 2 is usually left blank at this stage, but there is nothing to stop you putting a date in if you wish — the purchaser can always ask for an amendment. If you are including anything in the purchase price that you think needs specifying, complete Clause 7.

Get an original of your contract typed or written up with two carbon copies. Keep the original and send on the two unsigned copies to Skinner. In the fullness of time you will receive from the purchaser's solicitor his Enquiries Before Contract form Conveyancing 29 (LONG). Answer the questions in the same spirit of helpfulness as the vendor of registered land is instructed to do at page 90 to 92. He will no doubt be fully satisfied with your replies, but if he isn't, he will come back for more. In that case, reply to the best of your knowledge and ability.

Although it needn't be done until after contracts have been exchanged, enclose with the draft contract as much of the photo-copying of the deeds (conveyances) as you think will prove that you are the owner.

If your house is mortgaged the Building Society might send you a copy of a marked abstract. 'Marked' insofar as it will bear markings by a solicitor to say that the abstract has been compared with the original deeds which it summarises.

If you have the deeds in your possession do not, on any account, part with any at this stage.

Purchaser: You have viewed the house a couple of times and if you need a mortgage, you have got at least half a promise of one. You have bargained the price down with Feather, told him you are acting for yourself and given him your name and address. Receive the draft contract from your vendor's solicitor who may well not be as helpful as the vendor (above) and you may only receive the draft contract with a copy. Don't worry, he will give evidence of title later on. If you don't like the look of anything in the contract, give the vendor's solicitor a ring and agree the alterations you require and write them into the draft. The kind of things you are looking for are basically the same as for the purchaser of registered property (p.100-105).

The covenants are included in a conveyance, not necessarily the one to your vendor. *His* may only give the date and the parties to the conveyance in which the covenants *were* set out in full. Skinner must either set them out in full in the contract or supply you with a copy of them and refer to the conveyance from which they came, and if he doesn't, insist, because if you are a surgeon and there is a restrictive covenant against surging in or around the premises, you will not wish to waste further time and money on surveys and such like.

Land Registry: Send off search form 96 with a fee of £2. Give the address and either cut a piece out of a local street map or sketch a little plan of the surrounding streets to help with identification if you think the postal address might not be sufficient. When you get the form back it will reveal if there is a caution against first registration, and whether the land is registered or not (don't take the vendor's word on this — he might not know what he is talking about). If it is registered, you will be given the title number, and your task is much simpler from now on — you take your instructions from Chapter 11: Sale and Purchase of a Registered House. If in reply to form 96 they give you anything you don't understand, ring the enquiries department.

Land Charges form **K15**. Extract the name of your vendor and enter it together with his address in the spaces provided. Get from the contract the date your vendor bought, and enter that in the 'from' column. In the 'to' column put the year you are buying.

As you are sending off a number of forms keep the dates of their dispatch. Some come back by return of post, none should take more than a fortnight.

Your Building Society will require to know if you have been bankrupt. So together with your search form K.15 you can send an application for an Official Search (Bankruptcy Only) K16, provided that completion is not more than a fortnight ahead — lenders need up-to-date information. Put in the name/s of the intending borrowers, affix land registry stamps to the tune of 50p for each of the names to be searched on the K15 and K16 forms, and send them off to the address (Plymouth) on the back of the forms.

Usually the sending of form K15 is delayed until 14 days before completion because a certificate of search gives you protection for fifteen working days against anyone putting nasty things on the register. There is nothing to stop your searching twice or thrice if you wish, so you might as well find out as soon as possible about anything that needs clearing up or would be enough of a frightener to put you off the purchase. If the date protection ends, shown in the top right-hand box of the certificate of result of search you receive, is before completion date, send off another K15. It's well worth the bother.

For instance your vendors may not be as lovey-dovey as they appeared when they showed you round "Shangri-La", and if the house was bought in one name, the partner might have registered a Class F charge to protect matrimonial interests. You need to know about any Class F charge as soon as possible and certainly before you get too involved. If they have come to some arrangement about sharing the proceeds of the sale, so well and good. However, as soon as you receive your protection period certificate from Plymouth get an application to cancel the charge signed by the cautioner (See Chapter 14). A Building Society solicitor will expect you to produce the certificate on completion.

Couples do some barmy things when love turns, at best to indifference, at worst to hate. They often do all they can to make things difficult for the other side. If you had been buying a registered title the office copies would have wised you up on this problem. It is so that you don't get caught in the crossfire that I say: K15 to Land Charges Dept. as soon as possible, and certainly before you sign a contract.

It is all very well having a contract that is enforceable according to how the law is interpreted this week. But who wants the bother and expense of enforcement? And what if you came up against someone who thought that they and their case were something special, and it would be unjust for the law to be applied to them?

Such a situation has all the makings of a House of Lords case. *Having rights and asserting them are two vastly different things.* Possession really is nine points of the law! And another thing — always change the locks when you move in, particularly if the house has been standing vacant for any length of time.

Enquiries of District Councils (CON 29 A) or **Enquiries of Local Authority** (CON 29 D London, if your purchase is in a London Borough Council or the Corporation of London) together with **Search of Local Land Charges L.L.C.1:** Councils require you to provide two copies of each. Take them to the council as recommended at page 97. Both CON 29 A and CON 29 D LONDON forms are in two parts. If you want both parts answering it costs more. Fees are printed on the first part of the form. You must initial any of the questions in part 2 to which you need an answer. The kind of questions in part 2 are such as relate to public footpaths existing and contemplated, building preservation orders and so on, also questions about registration of houses in multiple occupation. If you initial any of them, look up the fee given on the form and add it to the standard fee.

The LLC1 form is printed in duplicate, one copy for the council to retain, and one to be returned to you with the answers. Use a carbon to complete. The local land charges register is divided into twelve parts, and the first question which faces you on the form is which parts you require searching. Strike out "Part(s) . . . of" and you will get the lot. It's much simpler, and costs very little more than picking and choosing. Like a lot of other things the prices keep moving up, but mercifully the charges are, in this instance, printed on the back of the form. The reference in the fees section of the form to "each parcel" means plots, so it does not concern the buyer of a single house.

Enquiries before Contract Form CON 29 (LONG): Send two copies to the Vendor's Solicitor.

If your vendor is a company (has Ltd. after its name) you need to be extremely careful that the company is not in the process of being wound up. If you are buying such a house that is *not registered* you should make a company search at Companies House, 5571 City Road, London EC1, either by calling there, or if it is too far away, by asking your C.A.B.* to give you the address of a land agent or credit reference agency who might help. The trouble here (and a solicitor is just as subject to it as you are) is that it takes time for a note of a winding-up petition to be put on a Company's file. Nevertheless, any sale made after winding-up proceedings have commenced is only a purported sale and is null and void. There are only two really safe ways to deal with such a case. The first is to have a director of the Company give his personal guarantee for the sale, and secure it on *his house*. The second is to insist that the vendor company gets the property registered before you sign your contract because this note on limited companies does *not* apply where the land is registered.

As the case where you are likely to come across a company as vendor is with a newly-built house, and it will be on an estate where the Registrar has already agreed to register the property, even though it is not in a compulsory area, the chance of your having to cope with this problem is extremely remote. It could occur in the case of a shop and house, because many small shopkeepers have been persuaded to trade as limited liability companies in the last couple of decades. In such cases caution is the order of the day. No matter what assurances people want to give — get some security out of them.

Vendor: Cope with any amendments to the contract, but don't be bullied into giving undertakings, or adding anything to the contract you don't fully understand. Keep asking for explanations and never be fobbed off with "it doesn't really mean what it says" or "it's usual, but doesn't matter/apply in this case". If it doesn't mean what it says or doesn't apply it may as well be struck out. On the other hand if *you* are asked to take something out and you are told "Oh, you don't need that in" you can riposte "Well, if

---

*Some C.A.B.s will even do the job for you.

you know it is doing no harm, you won't object to it remaining".

Purchaser: Receive the Enquiries before Contract form back from Skinner and glean from his answers what you can. If you are not satisfied, or suspect that he knows more than he is telling you, send him a few supplementaries in the form of a letter, but remember he was answering stock questions first time round so it should occasion little surprise that all you got in return were stock answers. He might slip in a note that *all* further enquiries must be received within . . . days. If you are taking a mortgage you can never be sure how many times your society's solicitor, Mr. O. Twist, will come back for more, so simply tell Skinner so. He will have to understand and withdraw the time limit.

Using the Enquiries before Contract form as a guide and pages 92 ff of The Sale and Purchase of a Registered House, carry out your inspection of the property and its environs, paying particular attention to the area of land within the fences, any facilities such as drives which are shared, and the neighbours' attitudes towards them.

If on inspection it turns out that the road leading to the house is badly potholed, it could be an indication that it is not maintained by the council because it is not adopted by them, so pay attention to Enquiries of Local Council. If it is a private road, after the description of the property in the contract it should say 'together with a right of way over the road coloured on the said plan'. On the other hand it might say the words "and the road has been taken over". Not to worry: of such redundancies are roots of title made up.

CON 29 A and LLC1 will come back from the Council with their printed answers. Check them through as at p.92. If replies on either form cause any head-scratching ask the person who wrote the replies what they mean. Council officials will always explain meanings, what they are not empowered to do is advise what should be done about them. But you never know. A remark such as "my goodness, I wonder what other chaps do in such a circumstance", might just elicit a useful hint of how to deal with a problem that is not simply of a technical nature.

By now, the Land Registry should also have returned your search of index map form 96 showing the house to be unregistered, but if there is any kind of entry it is your vendor's problem. Let him know, or to be more accurate, remind him, because he will almost certainly already be aware of the entry.

The reply to your K15 will come to you in the form of a Certificate of Result of Search. Whereas the Land Registry keeps a register of land and the name(s) of the owner(s) of each registered parcel of land, the Land Charges Department keeps a register of interests which third persons can have in an unregistered house, and which can be registered against the **names** of people. So if your vendor is called Tom Jones, the computer will throw up all the Tom Joneses known to it and you will have to decide which entries belong to your vendor. Luckily it also gives the addresses where the ubiquitous Joneses lived when the various charges were registered against them. If none of the entries apply to your vendor, he or his solicitor must write on the Certificate of Result of Search words to the effect that it is certified that none of the entries apply to him.

Obviously a bankruptcy charge would alert you to the fact that all is not well. More likely than not your reply will show "no entries". If there is one it is likely to be one of the following: C(i) This is a second (puisne) mortgage. D(ii) is a splatter of covenants which no doubt you already know of. "F" is a matrimonial home entry. One of the spouses, not being a joint owner, is protecting rights.

What do you do with any of these in the unlikely event of one or all showing up? In the case of C(i) second mortgage, as the reply you get will say no more than that the entry exists you write, quoting the date and reference number, to the Land Charges Registry, asking for a copy of the details. You need the details because on completion you will require the vendor's solicitor to produce the actual second mortgage deed duly receipted. Matrimonial Homes Class F we have already dealt with.

You will no doubt already know the contents of a D(ii) entry. The vendor or his solicitor should have put a copy with the draft contract. If he hasn't, ask him to bring the job to the top of the pile of "things to be done today".

By now you have sufficient knowledge to give you confidence to go forward, or back out of the deal. But have you sufficient funds? During all these to-ings and fro-ings between you and the vendor, you and the solicitor and you and the council, you have made an application to the Openhand Perpetual Building Society or Almoner's Bank Ltd.

The Mortgage

Things are changing rapidly in the mortgage business and lenders are recognising that it is a waste of their borrowers' money to have them pay solicitors twice for doing their work once. But at the moment of writing each society has what it calls a roll of solicitors to act for it on completion. You should be allowed to choose from a list, and your choice could then fall on the one who quotes the lowest price, and is likely to be the one who is also acting for your vendor. But more later about what happens with the building society solicitor.

So let us have a little re-cap of what a *purchaser* of an unregistered freehold house in England or Wales will have done up to this point. He will have:

Received the draft contract in duplicate with map.

Called at the Local Council and deposited LLC1 for information about the Council's interests in the property.

Sent or taken Form CON 29A or D to Council asking questions about roads, drains and restrictions on use.

Sent Form 96 to Land Registry to find out if registered, and if not, any cautions against first registration.

Sent Form CON 29 (LONG) Enquiries before Contract to Vendor's solicitor, attempting to find out what they know about any boundary disputes, rights of way, planning consents and such like.

It looks a pretty big list of forms, but you should be able to cope, particularly as nowadays solicitors seem to think nothing of taking two calendar months to get to the stage you are now at — I've seen houses built quicker. If you have managed to survive what's gone of this increasingly bureaucratic century, and are in a position mentally and financially to buy a house, the forms should not cause you any difficulty which, with the application of a little logic and commonsense, you can't solve for yourself.

Having received satisfactory replies, or your vendor being able to satisfy you on any points raised, you are now ready to exchange contracts, provided you have received a satisfactory mortgage offer from the Building Society.

Our Vendor, doing his own conveyance, has been told to send off copies of the previous conveyances with his draft contract. It seems a sensible way to do things, but sometimes solicitors acting for vendors will only send you the draft contract and won't let you have copy conveyances or an abstract of title (explained later) until contracts have been exchanged.

Note that in the contract the covenants will be either set out in full or reference made to their first appearance in the deeds and you should expect a copy of them (written out in full) before you sign the contract, and remember that if the covenants pre-date your vendor's ownership there is nothing you can do about them.

However, by now, all things having gone well, you can agree a completion date with the vendor. Enter it into the final copy (engrossed) contract, sign but do not date it and send to the Vendor's solicitor, together with the smallest deposit you have been able to get away with.

Vendor: Receive the contract signed by the purchaser, check that the deposit is with either a stakeholder or in a joint bank account. Enter the completion date on your copy, sign it, enter the date of your signing and send it off to the purchaser. You have got his part of the contract and he has got yours. Contracts are now said to be "exchanged".

If you have not already sent copies of the deeds and documents which prove your title, let Skinner have them now.

If you bought less than 15 years ago the only link in the title chain before the conveyance to you might be an abstract, and a solicitor will have endorsed it "Examined against the originals at the office..." This type of endorsed abstract is intended to be used as if it were a set of deeds when you come to sell, and any solicitor would accept it from a brother solicitor.

If in response Skinner sends some obscure requisitions (questions), answer fully, but be ready with the masterpieces:

Question: Who now holds the 1876 indenture?
Answer: I don't know.
Question: Was the plot conveyed in 1975 part of the one conveyed in 1920?
Answer: I suppose so.

If he persists in asking what this or that means give him "it means what it says". Eventually they give up what they should never have started.

Purchaser: Receive vendor's signed and dated part of the contract. Contracts are now said to be "exchanged" and the property is at the buyer's risk. So check that the contract is in the same terms as the one you signed and immediately arrange for the property to be fully insured with the same company as your lender will eventually use.

If you did not receive copies of the deeds (conveyances, etc.) you should expect them now. Check the conveyances watching for the points at page 122.

An abstract should show, in summary, an unbroken chain of ownership leading to your vendor. It might compress onto three or four pages the meat of a dozen conveyances, mortgage deeds, deeds of gift etc. In an abstract the full names and addresses of parties are not repeated over and over again. When an identical description of a property appeared in a subsequent deed it is referred to as "all the before abstracted premises". Exceptions and reservations are similarly treated, and wills are not set out in full, but only the date of the will and names of the executors are put in.

Abstracts of title are written in lawyer's speedhand which consists of abbreviations which are based on omitting vowels. However, Absd does not mean absurd but abstracted. Here are a few more abominations to be going on with: thereabouts: thrbts, vendor: vndr, property: ppty, hereditaments: hrdmts, indenture: indr, Solicitors: slrs, mortgage: mtge. You soon get a grsp of it but be crfl not to let it creep into your gnrl vcblry or it might be thought you need new dntrs.

Requisitions on Title form CON 28B should now be dispatched.

Vendor: Receive CON 28B. You only have to prove title going back 15 years. Remember that when you and previous owners bought, highly trained solicitors checked out the title so there can't be much if anything wrong with it. However, do your best and give the answers required in relation to providing a completion statement. This is an account showing the precise amount you will require to be paid when you hand the keys over and sign the conveyance. It is sufficient to let your local authority know the date when you are moving out and they will split the rate bill, and anything you have paid in advance will come back to you. Water Authorities are not always so obliging, so check with them and if necessary, show in your completion statement how much you need in order to reimburse you for the water rate paid in advance. So make up the bill and send it off with the completed CON 28B.

Purchaser: In reply to your Requisitions on Title you receive a list of the documents that will be handed over to you (or your lender) on completion and you are informed who will give a statutory acknowledgement and undertaking for the production and safe custody of any document of title not handed over. (This applies where, for instance, you are buying one of a block of terrace houses where the whole block previously belonged to a landlord. Obviously he can't and won't hand over the conveyance of the lot when you are only buying part, hence the statutory undertaking mentioned above). The form also asks for receipts for last payments of outgoings. Some purchasers' solicitors get all hot and bothered about whether the previous owner is doing a moonlight flit leaving the general rate unpaid. General rates are a personal debt on the occupier, so if any are outstanding for a period before you became the occupier, that debt does not belong to you — the council must look to your predecessor for payment. There is a space for further questions.

If the property is subject to compulsory registration check whether the "conditons of sale" on the back of the contract stipulates that the vendor's solicitor must produce all documents and information required for registration. If it doesn't, then get an undertaking from Skinner in those terms.

If you have raised some questions on the title and feel you haven't altogether got satisfactory answers, bear in mind two things. Firstly if the conveyance to your vendor looks all right, and the man described in there as the purchaser is now your vendor, then it *should* be all right, because he had a wizard of the law check out that his predecessors were all that they had cracked themselves up to be. Secondly, if you are taking a mortgage, the Building Society solicitor will make sure that you are getting good title, and he will keep on asking questions which you pass on to Skinner, until the Society is satisfied. After all, if you default in your payments and they have to sell the house to settle your account, they will only have as good a title (proof of ownership) as you got at this point.

You now prepare a draft of the "instrument of transfer" you intend to use. If your purchase lies in an area subject to compulsory registration use form 19 (or 19 JP if in joint names). At the top write 'Under Rule 72' and leave (6) blank for the vendor to fill in regarding covenants. If you are buying in joint names and you wish survivor to take all strike out "cannot" at (8). In layman's language the clause now reads . . . If between now and the next time the house is sold one of us dies the remaining partner/spouse is entitled to the whole of the sale price, on the strength of the survivor's signature alone. For (9) Certificate of Value, see below. The space for title number you leave blank because one has not yet been allocated by the registry.

If you are buying a new house on a development the builder's solicitor should provide the "instrument" form 20 or 43, because only part of the vendor's land is being transferred.

If your purchase is neither in an area of compulsory registration nor on a complex development where the developer has elected to register, your "instrument" will be a conveyance. **The specimen conveyance** shows the bare bones which you can use for your draft. All the information you require for 1. should come from your contract.

Any Law Stationer's will sell you engrossing paper and seals. But, by the way, let no one tell you it must all be typed. What you are doing was being done, and more elegantly, before typewriters were thought of.

Clause 3 of the specimen conveyance, certificate of value:

The reason why the specimen shows £20,000 at 1. (Certificate of Value) but £25,000 at 3. is to point out that you enter the top figure in the band in which your purchase falls. Above £40,000 the band is elastic so you need enter no figure.

Vendor: Receive and check the draft. Look for any deductions or additions that have been made to the one you got when you bought. If there are any with which you disagree, amend in *red ink* and bounce it back. Heed previous warnings about "Oh, it's usual" and "It doesn't mean what it says". If form 19, make sure that the covenants have been correctly entered at (6). When you are satisfied send it back marked "approved". But do not sign it. You do that when you get the money.

Purchaser: When your draft instrument of transfer comes back look for the red ink. It is extremely rare to find any but if you do, and you understand and accept, so well and good. If you don't accept, argue about it. If you don't understand, ask for an explanation as you are perfectly entitled to one. When you are satisfied write or type out a final copy. Prefer stout paper for a conveyance. After all it is to be *your* title deed. If it takes two or more separate sheets, punch three holes in the margin and bind together with tape. Stick wafer seals at signature points. Sign your instrument of transfer, have it witnessed and send it to Skinner so that he can have the vendor sign it ready for completion day.

From now on your job is basically the same as that handed out to the purchaser of a registered house. Just as he got his transfer form 19 approved — so you've got your conveyance approved. What differences there are only arise if you are taking a mortgage, and in relation to what your Building Society solicitor will want you to produce just before or on completion. The Building Society solicitor will, no doubt, have written to you asking for the following — even if he hasn't written, get them off to him as soon as you can and ask him if there is anything further required, because of the time limit there might be for asking questions on title.

1. Local Authority search forms and replies.

2. Enquiries before contract CON 29 (LONG).

3. Contract.

4. Copy conveyance received from vendor's solicitor.

5. Conveyance or form 19 to yourself (one of your copies).

6. Completed Land charges Form K15.

As most building societies don't return these documents, it is useful to keep copies for your use in future transactions.

The lender's solicitor will respond by sending you the mortgage deed, an account of fees and stamp duties, a sheet of requisitions on title and a list of the documents required to be handed over on completion. Deal with them as the purchaser of a registered property was instructed at p.111.

Stamps L(A) 451: Description of Instrument is answered with "conveyance" or "Land Registry form 19" as the case may be; the transferor is the vendor and you are the transferee. If you are buying any kind of building the postal address is sufficient; 6 is answered with "fee simple" for a freehold property where you are to be absolute owner/s. 7: put the same figure as in Certificate of Value. 7(f) tells you what (a) to (f) are looking for and your answers will usually be "none" as will be the case with 8, 9, 11 and 12. Sign at 10.

Stamps 61: The only document you present and describe is your "instrument of transfer".

Vendor: Receive the supplementary questions on title, and root about in the conveyances for answers not forgetting the time honoured "I cannot say", "I presume so" and other such masterpieces. If you have paid for the house all you are waiting for now is the money and you will have notified your purchaser of a suitable place for him to pay it over. If you still have a mortgage, completion will take place at your Building Society's solicitor's office whither the actual deeds will have been sent. On Form 28B you told him at 7E to whom you wanted the bank drafts making out. If you need the completion monies splitting between you and the Building Society or even between you, the Society and the vendor of the house you are now buying — say so.

Purchaser: Pass on the vendor's replies to your lender. You are now geared up for completion. Take with you:–

1. Mortgage deed ready signed by both of you if you are buying in joint names.

2. Bank draft if there is a balance of purchase price to pay in addition to deposit and mortgage monies.

3. Forms to be passed to Stamp Duty office after completion.

4. Authority for stakeholder to hand over deposit.

5. Unless you have got it agreed that a cheque will do, *cash* for any Insurance Guarantee premium, duties or fees that have not been added on to your loan, or worse still, might have been deducted.

The vendor's solicitor will produce:–

1. The vendor's title deeds.

2. Conveyance or Form 19 signed by vendor.

3. If vendor had a mortgage, his society's solicitor's undertaking to discharge it.

Vendor: Attend the venue for completion, taking along the keys, and the deeds. If you have a mortgage your deeds will still be with the lender. Most building societies will agree to deliver the deeds to your purchasers' solicitor, after completion, in exchange for a banker's draft made payable to the society, which you will collect on completion and send/take to the society after completion.

Purchaser: Attend completion. The vendor or his solicitor will be prepared to hand over originals of conveyances going back at least fifteen years, or any other documents that constitute the good root of title specified for in your contract and his epitome of title.

When the property you are buying has been split off a larger area you get a copy of the conveyance or other good root of title to your vendor which is certified "Examined with the original at the offices of Messrs. Skinner, Son & Skinner". It is as well to let the vendor's solicitor know exactly what you will expect to pick up at completion but the state of things being what it is most completions take place and the legal boys have not got all the documents together in time, so they give one another undertakings to produce them eventually. You can accept the same if otherwise it would cause a lot of running about *for you*, but take the precaution of adding time limits.

If what you are buying is being split off a larger area or block of property make sure that, if your purchase is not to be registered, a note of your purchase is written (endorsed) on the conveyance to your vendor: "By a conveyance dated ...... No.14 Plevna Place was conveyed to Mr. & Mrs. Bold". Again an undertaking that the other side will do it suffices, as you are getting possession and that's what really counts.

Skinner will then produce the conveyance or form 19 and you will briefly check that this is the self-same as you sent and that it has been signed by the vendor and witnessed.

You hand over an authority for the stakeholder to release the deposit, and if you are taking a mortgage you hand to the person representing the building society the documents you have briefly received from the vendor, together with: signed mortgage deed, stamp duty forms, money for extras such as Insurance premium, registration fees, and if for first registration a form 1A. (See p.143). Please note that even though your lender's solicitor is to send off the documents to the Land Registry for first registration, you are still doing the registering for yourself, and he is only acting as a post box because he cannot give you the bundle of deeds (one of which is now the mortgage deed you have executed), as they constitute the security for the loan.

If you are not taking a mortgage you can accept Skinner's undertaking to pay off Feather's mortgage but you will have wanted to see the Building Society's reply to his request for a redemption figure and will cunningly have had one of your bank drafts made payable to that building society whom you will natter until you get the deeds. When you do, you will have a proud look at them and search out Feather's mortgage to the society on the back of which there should be emblazoned the Building Society's seal and a form of receipt such as "The Openhand Perpetual Building Society hereby acknowledges receipt on or before the date hereinafter mentioned of all monies intended to be secured by the written Legal Charge the payment having been made by the within named borrower".

If a mortgage 1st, 2nd, 3rd or 93rd is to any other than a building society you want the deeds (conveyances and receipted legal charges) — no promises, no under-takings will do. The vendor will just have to get a bridging loan for a few days or Skinner will have to use his influence to put himself in a position to hand the deeds over to you on completion.

Compulsory Registration Areas

If you are buying in a compulsory registration area there is a little tidying-up job to do. If you are taking a mortgage the mortgagee will send the form and documents to the Land Registry. The form is a **1A**.

On page 1 enter the value and fee. The rate is: £18.00 for the first £12,000 plus £3 for every £2,000 and part thereof to £100,000, when it becomes £2 for every £10,000 above that. Top whack is £332 for one million and one pounds and over.

A registration fee is normally payable for registering a Legal Charge (mortgage) but when it is done at the same time as a first registration or a transfer for monetary consideration an abatement of fee applies, i.e. there is no fee to pay for registering the charge.

Page 2 needs care; leave in 1(a) if buying in one name (b) if you wish survivor to take all (c) if buying with a partner for business reasons etc. (d) if you are none of the above. If any of 3 applies make sure the vendor's solicitor or building society solicitor does it on completion. 4 is referring to certificates received in response to K15's. 6(a) to (d): you will know which you are. 7: on the dotted line put the date of your instrument of transfer if 1st part of statement doesn't (and usually it doesn't) apply. The "true" copy transfer or conveyance can be certified by you — no need to pay a solicitor. Page 3. No.1. Your own name and address, so that any nice conveyances written in copperplate on parchment come to you for lampshade-making. 2: describe the document as "Charge Certificate". In the schedule at the top of page 3 enter particulars of your mortgage. Where you are asked for a reference you can use your own initials/DIY.

Cash buyers: Strike out 2 at p.3. Make out form A13 in triplicate listing the documents and forms you are sending. Do not worry unduly whether you have sent all that the registrar will require because the vendor's solicitor must eventually provide. Copies you can certify for yourself with "I hereby certify this to be a true and correct copy".

You have now got yourself a house and may you enjoy many happy years there, surrounded by your loved ones and the splendid going-in presents your friends and relatives have bought for you.

Cash buyers will, in the fullness of time, receive their Land Certificate. Make sure you put a note of the title number in one or two safe places and put the certificate under the piano lid ready for the next time. Those with a mortgage receive a card from the Land Registry saying when the Charge Certificate will be issued, on which date send off an A44 putting '1' in box A, and for £3 get yourself a complete set of "office copies" of your deeds.

I hope you will have noticed that throughout this book the few dire warnings given have been about parting with your money for nothing, or making untested assumptions about what other people involved in your house buying and selling will do, won't do, will charge and won't charge.

So maybe a final caution will be acceptable. Your goal is to get the job done — your means are the best and easiest you can find. Your goal is not to do as "good a job" as solicitors do by aping their style and means. No matter how expert you try to make yourself look, no solicitor I have ever met will recommend you for an honorary law degree. Neither should any DIY conveyancer go lording it over those poor souls who do employ solicitors because they are, no doubt, already smarting – as do many who cannot, or dare not service their own cars, when faced with paying the hourly charges levied by garages. There are those who are capable but haven't, as yet, tried, and you will get more respect if you tell them what, at the end of the transaction you honestly feel about it, as I did years ago, saying, "I don't know what all the fuss was about, it will be a cakewalk next time!"

Specimen Conveyance

This Conveyance is made the   day of   19

BETWEEN the Vendors Xavier Lax and Susan Lax his wife both of 14, Plevna Place, Blossomton and the Purchasers Bernard Strong and Ivy Strong his wife both of 127, Lowfield Road, Blossomton.

WHEREAS The Vendor is the estate owner in fee simple in possession of the property hereby conveyed free from encumbrances except as hereinafter mentioned and has agreed with the purchasers for the sale to them of the property for the sum of £20,000 (twenty thousand pounds)

THIS DEED WITNESSETH

1.   That in consideration of the sum of twenty thousand pounds now paid by the purchaser to the vendor (the receipt of which the vendor hereby acknowledges) the vendor as beneficial owner hereby conveys to the purchaser ALL THAT land and property known as 14, Plevna Place, Blossomton as shown and outlined in red on the plan attached to a conveyance between Henry Feather and the vendor and dated the first of April 1971 and subject to the covenants therein contained TO HOLD the same unto the purchasers in fee simple as joint tenants in law and equity/tenants in common (decide)

2.   With the object of giving the vendor a full and sufficient indemnity but not further the purchasers hereby covenant with the vendors to observe fulfill and perform the above-mentioned covenants and indemnify the vendor against all actions and claims in respect thereof

3.   IT IS HEREBY CERTIFIED that the transaction hereby effected does not form part of a larger transaction or series of transactions in respect of which the amount or value or aggregate amount or value of the consideration exceeds £25,000.

IN WITNESS WHEREOF the parties have hereunto set their hands and seals the day and year first above written

SIGNED SEALED AND DELIVERED by (Vendor) (Seal)

in the presence of   (Witness)

SIGNED SEALED AND DELIVERED by (Purchaser) (Seal)

in the presence of   (Witness)

13. Selling Leasehold Property

If the house or flat you are selling is leasehold there are one or two things you have to do in addition to those in the Chapter "Selling a Registered House". The first is to peruse the property register included in your office copies and it will look something like this:-

SHORT PARTICULARS OF LEASE UNDER WHICH THE
LAND IS HELD
(the word lease includes a sub-lease)

			TERM		
DATE	PARTIES		YRS.	FROM	RENT
20.6.1972	1. Bradshaw Investments Limited		999	1.1.72	£5
	2. Sunshine Management Co. Ltd.				
	3. Clint Bold				*Premium*
					£6,500

NOTE A: - Lessor's title registered under XYZOO

The Registry might or might not have a copy of the original lease, but even if it has the Registrar is under no obligation to provide copies, although he has discretion, sparingly used, to furnish office copies if the original has been well and truly lost.

From the above and your lease, a copy of which you should have got from your solicitor when you bought, you can extract the information the purchaser or his solicitor will require.

Broadly follow my suggested contract given at p. 53 or 55 by keeping the first paragraph and clauses 1, 2, 3, 6 and 7 as they are and adjusting the other parts as follows:-

WHEREBY IT IS AGREED that the Vendors will sell and the purchasers will buy: the leasehold house Number 14, Sunshine Mansions, Blossomton, Edenshire, as the same is registered with good leasehold title at H M Land Registry under Title Number EDN98765 and was created by a lease dated 20.6.1972 for a term of 999 years for the sum of £20,000 (twenty thousand pounds).

Clause four now becomes: The property is sold subject to the restrictive covenants and matters referred to by or set out in entries on the charges and property registers and the terms rent reserved and lessees covenants contained in the said lease copies of the said lease and copies of the registers having been given to the purchasers' solicitor no questions shall be asked nor objections made in respect thereof.

Clause five becomes: The Vendors' title shall commence with the said lease and continue by office copies of Title No. EDN98765 which the Vendors will supply together with an authority to inspect the register.

The reason for Skinner needing an authority to inspect the register, even though you have provided him with office copies, is that he has to send an authority with his green form 94A just before completion in order to get himself the protection period.

Never be surprised at what solicitors will ask for when you are trying to keep your temper and with as little fuss and bother as possible put an anxious purchaser's mind at rest about whether he can become the next proud owner of your domain. For instance, Skinner might ask you for a copy of the landlord's title (he who is lord of the actual soil — the free-holder — or the lessor — underlessor, take your pick). If you have a copy in the file under the piano lid let him have it (the copy) or if the person you pay the rent to will come across with an authority to inspect the register get one, in cases where the Lessor's title is registered. They aren't always registered, in which case, there is nothing anyone can do about it, so just smile and tell Skinner he will have to do without, as did apparently the solicitors you paid to act for you when you bought and the solicitors acting for the Openhand Perpetual did and then advised their society that the security was good enough for your mortgage.

I have conveyed a number of flats, all in the same block. All had the same title, all had the same lease, but the purchasers' solicitors all had different questions. Things that one solicitor thought to be of crucial importance others completely ignored and chose others to create a great song and dance about, while others accepted everything at face value. All paid over their client's money eventually. There's a lesson in that somewhere and not only for do-it-yourself conveyancers.

14. *Matrimonial Homes*

Hitherto, care has been taken not to offend half the population by giving the impression that only the male sex is capable of understanding and coping with a property deal. Hence the use of the all-purpose "person", or "spouse", and sometimes leaving the reader to decide whether Skinner was Mr., Mrs., Miss or Ms. But in this chapter taking the risk of giving unintended offence, such general terms will be abandoned. It will be assumed that we are dealing with property where the ownership is vested solely in the husband's name and a claim to have the house treated as the matrimonial home is being made by the wife. This is done for two reasons: Firstly because clarity demands it, and secondly because it corresponds to the situation in the real world. However, any husband who needs to protect his interests in a house that was "put in the wife's name" will not find it too difficult to transpose the term "husband" for "wife", and vice versa as necessary.

A wife might not be certain whether the house was in fact purchased jointly by her and her husband. If there is a mortgage it's easy — ask the building society. In other cases ask the solicitor who acted. If you suspect that the solicitor might be afraid of breaching confidence (or, is biased towards your husband) make the enquiry in writing because if it *is* in joint names then as you paid half the solicitor's costs you have a right to any information in his file. For him to refuse you the information is naughty and he knows it. A wife who knows or learns that the house was bought in joint names is fully protected. The house cannot be sold or mortgaged without her consent, nor can she be evicted without a court order — such a wife need read no further except out of curiosity and academic interest.

Reference here to "the Act" will be to the Matrimonial Homes Act 1967 as amended by the Matrimonial Proceedings and Property Act 1970. The purpose of the Act was to protect the right of a wife to occupy the matrimonial home. Once a wife registers her right in the appropriate register all intending purchasers and lenders of money on mortgage will have notice of her rights and they continue negotiations at their peril until they have the written assurance that the wife will agree to withdraw her charge from the register.

But before sending off forms in all directions, the wife needs to establish whether her husband is owner, tenant, or holds the property on lease. In the case of a leaseholder, unless the lease was for more than 21 years when it was granted, it is incapable of registration, and is a short tenancy. Even so, a wife cannot be evicted without a court order.

Another simple point, but worth making, just in case, is that before a wife can protect her interest in and right to occupy the house, her husband must have a right of occupation. Wives' rights of occupation arise on the latest of the following events:-

1) The date when the husband acquired the house
2) The date of the marriage, or
3) 1st January, 1968

It is no good trying to register a wife's interest if a contract of sale has already been signed nor will her registration affect any first mortgages, or further mortgages that have been made and registered before her application, although in the case of a second mortgage she might be protected under Section 70(1)(g) of the Land Registry Act — see the C.A.B. or a solicitor.

So how does one go about registering an interest? As you have already suspected it is a matter of form-filling again. (Forms are obtainable from HM Stationery office or OYEZ Stationers). It is something you can do easily and cheaply for yourself. Where you do not know whether the house is registered or not send off form 96 to the Land Registry for your area with "This search is being made solely for the purposes of the Matrimonial Homes Act, 1967" written across the top, and no charge will be made.

You will get a reply within a day or two telling you whether it is registered or not; if it is registered you will be given the title number. You then send off form 99 with a fee of £1, preferably Land Registry stamps (obtainable from a Post Office) but a cheque or postal order could be used if you feel the matter is urgent, and the deed is done. The registrar does not inform your husband of the registration — but you might think it civilised to inform him, just in case he is in negotiation with some unsuspecting person who is about to have his time and money wasted.

In the case of an unregistered house the required form is a K2, which is sent to the Land Charges Department, Burrington Way, Plymouth PL5 3LP no matter where the house is situate. The fee in this case is 50 pence and you will be informed within a day or two that a class F land charge has been registered in your name. Again, your husband will not know unless you tell him.

Where you suspect that dealings are imminent and the time taken in the to-ing and fro-ing outlined above might be too long for safety, I suggest you assume both that it is, and that it isn't registered. Send a form 96 as recommended above and pin it to a form 99 with your pound. On the form 99 in the box for the title number write "please supply title number for purpose of Matrimonial Homes Act 1967. URGENT". At the same time send off a form K2 with its 50p fee to Plymouth. That's belt and braces for you!

Once you've got a charge on a register (or both as in the previous paragraph) basically it stays there until death or divorce you do part, and it is known as a charge, and constitutes a caution against dealing. Nevertheless, a judge can make what is known as a "continuation order" of the wife's right of occupation which can now continue even though the marriage is at an end. But note, though the judge has said so, it does not mean that the whole world has notice. The charge did die with the marriage, so get a copy of the judge's order from the court office quickly and attach it to a form 100 in the case of a registered house or K.8 if the house is unregistered. Post form 100 with £1 fee to the Land Registry or K.8 with 50p to Plymouth Land Charges Department. If you hadn't for any reason got a charge onto one of the registers before the Court hearing then you must get a form 99 or K.2 off as swiftly as possible as explained above.

Judges don't always make continuation orders — the reverse may happen — he may order that the right of occupation is at an end. In this case a copy of the order with a letter from the husband is sufficient if the property is registered. No fee is required to have the Charge removed at the appropriate Land Registry.

In the case of unregistered land, you need to send the evidence, a covering letter, and a form K.13 together with a fee of 50p to the Land Charges Department, Plymouth, to have the class F Charge removed from the register.

A wife may apply to have the registration removed at any time by sending a letter to the Land Registry, or in the case of an unregistered house, form K.13 with a fee of 50p to the Land Charges Department.

Once a wife's right of occupation is registered it does no more than ensure that the house is not sold or mortgaged except with her consent or a court order. When a wife is in occupation she can achieve the same end, for some time, by simply refusing to show viewers or building society and finance company surveyors round the property. No lender will want to lend, and no purchaser will want to negotiate for a property that has such an uncooperative person living in it.

A wife can only protect her right of occupation in respect of one house, so if her husband owns more than one she will register her right for the one she prefers.

A registration of right to occupy says nothing about how

the proceeds will be divided if and when the house is sold. It is essential that the parties try to find a solution between themselves on this point. Recourse to the courts should be the very last resort. Costs can be ruinous, and you might eventually have to pay them yourself, even though you were granted legal aid, because only the first £2,500 of the proceeds of litigation are exempt from the power of the Legal Aid Fund to recover its own contribution. A person who lodges a caution without reasonable cause is liable in damages to anyone injured as a result.

Where the husband thinks the wife, or person who had a charge registered had no right to do so, he can write to the Registrar at the appropriate Registry and ask to have the Cautioner "warned off". The Registrar then gives the cautioner (wife) notice that before the expiration of notice (usually 14 days) she must show cause why the caution should continue to have effect. She can write, have her solicitor write, or appear before the Chief Registrar. Failure to do one of these things means that at the expiration of the notice the caution will cease to have effect.

Earlier, purchasers were advised to treat all cautions (which include all class F and Matrimonial Charges of course) with grave suspicion, so you will realise that the sooner cautions are removed, the better.

When an armistice is being arranged, consider putting in a condition that the house be put in joint names (transfer of ownership by way of gift). Whether registered or unregistered land it's only a two minute job. If it's unregistered but in a compulsory registration district you might consider registering it at the same time — D.I.Y. conveyancers prefer registered property and it might just tip the scales if ever you need to sell quickly.

Relations with Solicitors

Solicitors have a legal monopoly of conveyancing *for a fee*. But as more and more people follow the example of friends who are now qualified DIY conveyancers, those in the legal profession seem to be reconciling themselves to losing their monopoly.

Solicitors used to think that DIY conveyancers spelled trouble, but experience has proved otherwise. Moreover, in a litigious age, there is an increasing amount of other work which only lawyers can do. The snag is that they are not allowed to advertise for it, so on the occasions when his work does bring him into contact with normal people (property-owning democrats) the forward-looking lawyer thinks, "I may not be getting a conveyance out of this person, but later perhaps a will, trust, divorce or libel action will be coming and this person could have the spending of all that lovely money or be able to tell someone who has – 'I know a very bright, pleasant and efficient firm'".

Coda

The term land owner or property owner used to refer to the possessor of numerous farms and vast tracts of land or row after row of houses and factories, so one can readily understand why such a person needed estate agents to manage and solicitors to transact his affairs for him.

The mushrooming of "estate agents" and "solicitors" shops all over the place in the last fifty years merely to handle the affairs of people who own only a few square yards of land with a little house on it is unnecessary, ridiculous and expensive for owner-occupiers who are struggling to make ends meet.

For a *lawyer* to spend his time on undefended divorce and conveyancing is to misuse his training, expertise and the status that he has achieved and the community ascribes to a person in his position. Every *lawyer* worthy of his proud title proves the point because as soon as his practice is large enough such work is delegated to clerks and he goes on to do the work for which he was trained — law.

15. Did You Know?

THAT If you are to appear in court on a criminal charge unless it is of a very trivial nature you should get a solicitor quickly. In a serious case, a man who plays at being his own lawyer usually has a fool for a client. Legal aid is always available in criminal cases although it is not necessarily free, the accused may be required to make a contribution.

THAT if you give part or all of your house to a loved one, say, your child, husband, wife or lover without receiving money, rendering the transfer legal will only take a few minutes of your time. You are legally entitled to do it yourself and there is no need to drag yourself to Skinner, Blood and Stone's office. A few forms and a small registration fee suffice. See list at back of book.

THAT the maximum loan a husband and wife team can claim tax relief on is £30,000. But provided the individuals are not married then each can claim relief on up to £30,000 of a loan, provided they both live in the house and are joint owners.

THAT if you bought a house before the date when compulsory registration was extended to the area you live in you are under no obligation to register it now. It *will have to be registered* by whoever purchases it from you. If however, you think that do-it-yourself conveyancing is rapidly becoming the in thing and that purchasers might rather do the conveyance on a registered than an unregistered house you might do what you are perfectly entitled to do now — register your ownership. If the house is mortgaged you will obviously need the consent and co-operation of your building society. The dealings with the Land Registry need only one Form A4, then follow the instructions given at the end of the chapter on The Sale and Purchase of an Unregistered House.

THAT If you are a leaseholder and pay an annual rent for the privilege of your house standing on someone else's land and the lease has a long time to run (say over fifty years) the freeholder might sell if you offer him about a twelve year purchase e.g. rent £20 per annum times twelve equals £240.

THAT If you think that the rates you have to pay are too high in comparison with what other owners of similar properties are paying you can appeal. If it comes to a hearing before the Local Valuation Court (consisting of three local worthies) it involves you in no costs unless you take a professional adviser along with you in which case you will be responsible for his fee.

THAT Anybody can find out the value of an estate. Anybody can get a copy of a will. That is why newspapers can publish. Of course it can't be done until the testator is dead and probate of the will granted. Write to the Principal Registry of the Family Division, Somerset House, Strand, London WC2R 1LD and enclose £2 for the Record Keeper.

THAT If a slate falls from your roof onto the head of a passer-by it's no use pleading 'Act of God'. He has a claim against you for nuisance or negligence and hopefully you have insurance to cover you. In any case the injured party might be an atheist.

THAT You are committing no offence if you take mushrooms, blackberries or flowers that are growing wild. But you will be, if you take the plants, as you will if you sell the produce you have so painstakingly gathered. Going onto someone else's land you have certainly committed a trespass, which is a civil wrong and the owner can claim from you for any damage you have done. So if when you arrived there were blackberries on the bushes and when you propose leaving there are not, the owner of the land or his agent (ask for proof of identity) can ask for the produce in payment for the damage.

THAT You cannot get tax relief on an overdraft even if you can prove that the loan was taken out for the purchase or improvement of a property. The loan must be by way of a loan account to qualify.

THAT If your neighbour's tree overhangs your garden you may cut off the offending branches, but you must give him the cuttings because they belong to him.

THAT You must be extremely careful not to get into boundary disputes with your neighbour. They are extremely difficult to settle. Most lawyers don't want the business because most of their clients simply do not have the kind of money (hundreds and hundreds) that would pay the bills that are so easily run up. At the scale to which plans are drawn in deeds and registered titles the inked line itself covers at least a foot if not a yard.

If your neighbour insists on making trouble let it be he who traipses off to a solicitor. Let it be he whom the solicitor warns that he could be hazarding a lot of hard-earned money. The solicitor will certainly try the old ploy of sending you a letter threatening you with damnation and virtual destruction if you don't let his client have all his own way. Treat the letter with a pinch of salt unless you happen to know that your neighbour is extremely rich and can afford to keep his lawyer in the style to which he aspires. In that case call in at your local Citizens Advice Bureau for their advice.

THAT There are no official registers from which you can learn who owns vacant land or derelict property. All you can do is ask around. Local parsons and old established doctors are likely sources of information.

THAT You don't need to employ a solicitor to apply for

probate or letters of administration. If the deceased left a will any of the executors can make application, and if no executor is to be found then any person who has an interest in what was left can apply at the local probate registry (address in telephone book or local C.A.B.).

In cases where the deceased left no will then the persons who can apply are in the following order of preference:

(1) widow or widower (2) child (3) parent (4) brother or sister (5) others having an interest.

THAT When you have paid a solicitor his bill you are entitled to have handed to you the whole of the file referring to the work he has done for you.

THAT Whenever you move into a house it is prudent to have the locks changed. When the house has been left vacant and keys for viewing handed out, it is imperative.

THAT the piece of road outside your house is intended for travelling on so you cannot complain if someone else parks on it just when you wanted to...

But say you have a garage or parking space alongside your house and some one parks in such a way that your access is restricted then he is committing a criminal offence of obstruction and you can bring the police to him. He is also committing the civil offence of nuisance and you could have a go at him in the county court. If the same person committed the nuisance regulary it might be worth your while to sue him. In any case, always be careful when parking on the road side that *your* car is not in a position to impede a fire engine at work. Firemen have to work quickly and decisively! You don't want them to go to work on unceremoniously moving away your pride and joy!

THAT there is a difference between an estimate and a quotation. If a builder gives you an estimate of £100 for a job the bill could turn out to be anything around £10 either side. But a quotation is firm; if the quote is £100 then the bill should be the same. However, always make sure that you get a quote for *everything* that is to be done - - - it is the unquoted-for extras that you decide to have done during the course of the work that always turn out to be costly.

THAT no one - - - absolutely no one can be evicted from any kind of property of which he is the tenant or owner (even if he apparently only owns five per cent and has a mortgage for the rest) without a Court order having been made; a Court order cannot be applied for until a written notice giving at least one month's notice to quit has expired in the case of a tenancy.

THAT if the Gas Council or the Electricity Area Board cut off your supply and can't prove a good reason for their action you can prosecute them in the Magistrates' court and if you win they will be fined.

THAT if you are fed up with the cry, "Missus can I have my ball back", that if you touch the ball you must legally give it back to your tormentor and owner, but if you allow the ball to lie where it is the owner has no right to come into your garden to retrieve it.

THAT it is not your duty to fence out animals. It is up to the owners of animals (cattle, horses, goats, pigs, elephants and poultry) to fence them in. If they stray and trespass their owner is liable for the damage they do.

HOWEVER if your dog is the cause of an accident on the highway you will be liable unless you can prove that you always keep the dog under control i.e. fenced in, but some twerp had left the gate open which was clearly marked "keep closed at all times", or that you kept the dog on a lead, but unbeknown to you he had been taking lessons in escapology.

CATS can go and do as they please without their owner having to stump up.

DOGS get their owners into real cash trouble if the owner sets the dog on some destructive course.

THAT It is best to have a look at the section on liability for animals in "Charlesworth", one of the major legal reference books on negligence, before committing yourself to spending money on prosecuting or defending such a claim. See Charlesworth at your local reference library or nearest University or Polytechnic. Walk up to the nearest librarian and ask to be directed to the book. You will never be refused.

THAT Rent charges — sometimes known as "chief rents" in the North of England and "ground rents" in the West of England are not the same as the annual payments made to a lessor for a lease as in the chapter "Selling Your Leasehold House or Flat".

BUT If you pay a rent charge (more often than not in the region of £5 to £10 per year) you are entitled to redeem it for approximately ten times the amount of the annual charge. So for a matter of between fifty and one hundred pounds you can rid yourself of the yearly chore of paying and all the tedious questions Skinner & Probe will love to ask you when you come to want to sell. Application forms from Department of Environment, 2 Marsham Street, London, SW1P 3EB.

THAT If you are too busy to do your own conveyance you should ring round the local Skinners and ask for quotations. As stamp duties, search and other fees are standard and known as disbursements, what you are trying to find out is how much Skinner will charge for his work. So if he starts rotting on about fees for this, that and the other cut him short and ask — how much in addition to your disbursements? On the sale of a £20,000 house and the purchase of one at £21,000, quotations have ranged from £300 to £750. If Skinner spots that you are asking round and tells you that you are wasting your time because the local branch of the law society have come to an arrangement, keep on ringing round because if he is not pulling *your* leg they might be pulling *his!*

THAT There is no lawyer by the name of Skinner in a practice which has the name Skinner in its business name, and even if there were we are not referring to him nor any person by the name of Skinner who has or has ever had a certificate to practise law.

Appendix I Land Registry Addresses

AREAS SERVED BY THE DISTRICT REGISTRIES OF
H.M. LAND REGISTRY as on 1 APRIL 1981

A local area supplement to this list is available free from district land registries.
It shows in greater detail the operative date of compulsory registration of districts.

County	*Districts subject to compulsory registration*	*District Land Registry*
AVON	Bath Bristol Kingswood	Plymouth
BEDFORDSHIRE	Luton North Bedfordshire South Bedfordshire	Stevenage
BERKSHIRE	wholly compulsory	Gloucester
BUCKINGHAMSHIRE ...	South Bucks	Stevenage
CAMBRIDGESHIRE	Cambridge Peterborough	Peterborough
CHESHIRE.	wholly compulsory	Birkenhead
CLEVELAND	wholly compulsory	Durham
CLWYD	wholly non-compulsory	Swansea
CORNWALL	wholly non-compulsory	Plymouth
CUMBRIA	Barrow-in-Furness	Durham
DERBYSHIRE	Bolsover Chesterfield Derby Erewash South Derbyshire	Nottingham
DEVON	East Devon Exeter Plymouth South Hams Teignbridge Torbay	Plymouth
DORSET	Bournemouth Christchurch Poole Weymouth and Portland Wimborne	Plymouth
DURHAM	Chester-le-Street Darlington Durham Easington Sedgefield	Durham
DYFED	Llanelli	Swansea
EAST SUSSEX	wholly compulsory	Tunbridge Wells

County	District subject to compulsory registration	District Land Registry
ESSEX	Basildon Brentwood Epping Forest Harlow Southend-on-Sea Thurrock	Stevenage
GLOUCESTERSHIRE	Gloucester	Gloucester
GREATER LONDON	Bexley Bromley Croydon Greenwich Kingston upon Thames Lambeth Lewisham Merton Richmond upon Thames Southwark Sutton Wandsworth	Croydon
	Barnet Brent Camden City of London City of Westminster Ealing Enfield Hackney Hammersmith and Fulham Haringey Harrow Hillingdon Hounslow Inner Temple and the Middle Temple Islington Kensington and Chelsea Tower Hamlets	Harrow
	Barking Dagenham Havering Newham Redbridge Waltham Forest	Stevenage
GREATER MANCHESTER ...	wholly compulsory	Lytham
GWENT	Islwyn Newport	Swansea
GWYNEDD...	wholly non-compulsory	Swansea
HAMPSHIRE	Eastleigh Fareham	Weymouth
	Gosport Havant New Forest Portsmouth Southampton	Weymouth
HEREFORD AND WORCESTER	Bromsgrove Hereford Worcester	Swansea
HERTFORDSHIRE	wholly compulsory save for the districts of Dacorum and North Hertfordshire	Stevenage

County				Districts subject to compulsory registration	District Land Registry
HUMBERSIDE	...	...	...	Cleethorpes E. Yorkshire Great Grimsby Kingston upon Hull Scunthorpe	Durham
ISLE OF WIGHT	...	...	...	wholly non-compulsory	Weymouth
KENT	...	...	...	wholly compulsory	Tunbridge Wells
LANCASHIRE	...	...	...	Blackburn Blackpool Burnley Fylde Preston Rossendale	Lytham
LEICESTERSHIRE		...	...	Blaby Charnwood Hinckley and Bosworth Leicester North West Leicestershire Oadby and Wigston	Peterborough
LINCOLNSHIRE	...	...	...	Lincoln	Peterborough
MERSEYSIDE	...	...	...	wholly compulsory	Birkenhead
MID-GLAMORGAN		...	...	Ogwr Rhondda Taff-Ely	Swansea
NORFOLK	...	...	...	Norwich	Peterborough
NORTHAMPTONSHIRE		...	...	Kettering Northampton	Peterborough
NORTHUMBERLAND	...		...	Blyth Valley Wansbeck	Durham
NORTH YORKSHIRE	...		...	York	Durham
NOTTINGHAMSHIRE	...		...	wholly compulsory save for the districts of Bassetlaw and Newark	Nottingham
OXFORDSHIRE	...	...	...	Oxford South Oxfordshire Vale of White Horse	Gloucester
POWYS	...	...	...	wholly non-compulsory	Swansea
SALOP	...	...	...	wholly non-compulsory	Swansea
SOMERSET	...	...	...	wholly non-compulsory	Plymouth
SOUTH GLAMORGAN	...		...	wholly compulsory	Swansea
SOUTH YORKSHIRE	...		...	wholly compulsory	Nottingham
STAFFORDSHIRE	...		...	Cannock Chase Lichfield Newcastle-under-Lyme Stoke-on-Trent Tamworth	Nottingham
SUFFOLK	...	...	...	Ipswich	Peterborough
SURREY	...	...	...	wholly compulsory	Tunbridge Wells

County			Districts subject to compulsory registration	District Land Registry
TYNE AND WEAR	...	...	wholly compulsory	Durham
WARWICKSHIRE	...	...	wholly compulsory save for the district of Stratford-on-Avon	Gloucester
WEST GLAMORGAN	...	...	wholly compulsory	Swansea
WEST MIDLANDS	...	...	wholly compulsory	Gloucester
WEST SUSSEX	...	...	... wholly compulsory save for the district of Chichester and Horsham	Weymouth
WEST YORKSHIRE	...	...	wholly compulsory	Nottingham
WILTSHIRE	...	...	... wholly non-compulsory	Plymouth

The following are the postal addresses and telephone numbers of the district land registries referred to in the foregoing list.

BIRKENHEAD
The Birkenhead District Land Registry
76 Hamilton Street, BIRKENHEAD,
Merseyside L41 5JW
(Telephone: 051-647 5661)

CROYDON
The Croydon District Land Registry
Sunley House, Bedford Park
CROYDON CR9 3LE
(Telephone: 01-686 8833)

DURHAM
The Durham District Land Registry
Aykley Heads, DURHAM DH1 5TR
(Telephone: Durham (0385)
61361/41516)

GLOUCESTER
The Gloucester District Land Registry
Bruton Way, GLOUCESTER GL1 1DQ
(Telephone: 0452 28666)

HARROW
The Harrow District Land Registry
Lyon House, Lyon Road, HARROW,
Middx HA1 2EU
(Telephone: 01-427 8811)

LYTHAM
The Lytham District Land Registry
LYTHAM ST. ANNES, Lancs. FY8 5AB
(Telephone: Lytham (0253) 736999)

NOTTINGHAM
The Nottingham District Land Registry
Chalfont Drive, NOTTINGHAM NG8
3RN
(Telephone: Nottingham (0602) 291111)

PETERBOROUGH
North Minster Rd., PETERBOROUGH
PE1 1XN
(Telephone: 0733 46048)

PLYMOUTH
The Plymouth District Land Registry
Plumer House, Tailyour Road,
Crownhill, PLYMOUTH PL6 5HY
(Telephone: Plymouth (0752) 701234)

STEVENAGE
The Stevenage District Land Registry
Brickdale House, Danestrete
STEVENAGE, Herts. SG1 1XG
(Telephone: Stevenage (0438) 4488)

SWANSEA
The Swansea District Land Registry
37 The Kingsway, SWANSEA SA1 5LF
(Telephone: Swansea (0792) 50971)

TUNBRIDGE WELLS
The Tunbridge Wells District Land
Registry, TUNBRIDGE WELLS, Kent
TN2 5AQ
(Telephone: Tunbridge Wells (0892)
26141)

WEYMOUTH
The Weymouth District Land Registry
1 Cumberland Drive, WEYMOUTH
Dorset DT4 9TT
(Telephone: Weymouth (03057) 76161)

ADVERTISEMENTS, 6, 7

APPLICATION FOR OFFICE COPIES, *see OFFICE COPIES*

AUCTION, 13, 25, 176

AUTHORITY TO INSPECT, 52, 64, 85, 88, 108, 114

BANK, 3

BANKRUPTCY, 62, 96, 133
    Search, 16, 62

BANKER'S DRAFT, 82, 92, 116, 117, 119, 141, 143

BENEFICIAL OWNER, 50, 100

BOARD, For Sale, 6

BUILDING SOCIETY —
    Insurance Guarantee, 42
    Solicitor, 107, 108, 111-13, 138, 139, 141
    Seal, 143
    Form of receipt, 143
    Surveyor, 30, 41

BUILDING —
    Regulations, 61, 104
    Extension, 70

BOUNDARIES, *also see VIEWING*
    Fences, 67
    Disputes, 90, 93

CAVEAT EMPTOR, ix, 80

CAUTION *(see also CHARGE)*, 72, 74, 105
    Release, 106
    Against first registration, 128

CERTIFICATE OF VALUE, 140

CERTIFIED COPY, 144

CHARGE —
        Certificate, 61, 63, 67, 68, 115, 118
    Legal, 70, 111
    Discharge of, 111, 153

COGNITIVE DISSONANCE, 5

CONTINUATION ORDER, 153

CONTRACTS, 16, 47ff, 79, 88
    Binding, 56
    Conditional, 58
    Conditions, 48, 50, 58, 124

Consideration, 47
Draft, 47, 67, 79, 85, 88, 100, 123, 127
Enquiries before, 80, 89-92, 127
Exchange of, 49, 85, 105, 107, 135
For registered land, 53, 83, 85
For unregistered land, 55, 123, 127
Leasehold, 147, 148
New houses, 38
Parties to, 47
Points to check, 100, 105-6
Subject to, 2, 38, 87
Signature, 82, 106
Time the essence, 50
Unconditional, 60

CONVEYANCE
Copy of, 135
Draft, 138, 139
Gibson on, 94, 121
Gift by way of, 123
Last one, 122
Originals, 142
Originals examined, 142
Specimen, 138, 146

COMPLETION, 141
Date, 38, 49, 56, 57, 91, 106
Delayed, 49, 107
Notice to, 49, 82, 84
Statement, 110, 113, 116
Mortgaged property, 141

COMPANIES (Ltd), 131

COMPULSORY PURCHASE ORDER, 61

COVENANTS, 124, 126, 135
Breach of, 69, 103
Recited, 126
Restrictive, 33, 38, 51, 62, 67, 102
Waived, 70

DEPOSIT, 2, 3, 40, 49, 82, 100, 106
Cheque, 106
Holding, 100
Release of, 84, 117, 119
Vendor's use, 100

DEEDS, 45
Endorsed summary, 126
Lost, 63
Obtaining, 124

Plan, 94
Splitting, 142

DEVELOPMENT MAP, 97
Complex, 138

DEVISE, 123

DISPUTES, 93

DOCUMENTS, list of, 144

DRAINS, 28, 92
Septic tank, 95, 99
Testing, 29

ELECTRICITY, 27, 94

ENGROSSING PAPER, 121

ENQUIRIES —
Before contract, 80, 85, 89, 90, 131, 132
Local authority, 61, 96, 98, 103, 130

EPITOME OF TITLE, 124, 127

EXCEPTIONS and RESERVATIONS, 135

ESTATE AGENTS, 10ff, 14
Organisations, 11
Instructions, 16, 55

EXECUTOR, 101, 136

EXTRAS, 57, 101
Inventory, 51

FEE SIMPLE, 123, 140

FITTINGS, 5, 51, 101

FIXTURES, 5, 51, 101

FOOTPATHS, 130

FOR SALE BOARD, 6

FREEHOLD, 33, 52, 101, 123

GAS, 94

GAZUMP, 2, 56

GRANTS, 43, 104

HEIRS INTENDED, 123

HOME LOAN SCHEME, 39

IMPROVEMENT GRANT, 104

INDEMNITY, insurance, 68

INLAND REVENUE —
Stamp office, 119, 121
'Stamps 61' Form, 140
Particulars delivered L(A)451, 113, 119
Completing, 140

INSTRUMENT, description of, 113, 122
of transfer, 138

INSURANCE —
Mortgage Protection, 44, 45
of property, 104, 135
Fire, 104
Rebate of premium, 107
Guarantee premium, 143
Interest late completion, 52, 102

JOINT NAMES, 109, 138

JOINT TENANTS, 109

KEYS, 83, 84, 85, 119

LAND CHARGES DEPT., 61, 96, 133

LAND CERTIFICATE, 45, 79, 84, 85, 87, 116, 118
Lost, 63

LAND REGISTRY, ix, 61
Charges register, 63, 65, 66
Guarantee of title, 62
History, ix, 62-63
Property register, 63, 65
Proprietorship register, 63, 65
Stamps, 79, 87, 152
Title number, 68, 87, 89
Registration compulsory, 62, voluntary, 63

LEASEHOLD, 52, 65, 123
Title, 65
Rents, 33

LEGAL AID, 154

LESSOR, 65

LOCAL COUNCIL, 61
Rating, 78

LETTERS OF ADMIN., 101, 124

LOAN, 100, 106, 143
  Bridging, ix, 3

MAINTENANCE CHARGES, 33

MORTGAGE, 40ff
  Bank, 44
  Building society, 40
  Deed, 140
  Discharge of, 111, 116
  Insurance guarantee, 42
  Maximum advances, 101
  Offer, 105
  Puisne, 133
  Redemption, 111, 119, 120, 143
  Retention, 42
  Second, 61, 143
  Tax relief, 43

MORTGAGEE: in possession, 50

MORTGAGOR, 50

MATRIMONIAL HOMES, 61, 72, 105
  Charge Class F, 129, 133, 152

MISREPRESENTATION, 90

MULTIPLE OCCUPATION, houses in, 130

NATIONAL HOUSEBUILDING COUNCIL, 31, 32, 37, 90

NEW HOUSES, 36ff
  Discounts, 39
  Exchange schemes, 39
  Transfer form, 138

NUISANCE, 68

OFFICE COPIES, 48, 52, 63, 64
  Application for, 79
  Complete set, 87
  Date stamp, 75, 85, 88, 114
  Registry entries, 119

OVERRIDING INTERESTS, 91, 92, 106

PARCELS (PLOTS), 130

PERSONAL REPRESENTATIVE, 51

PLAN, 48, 101, 123, 126
  Filed, 75, 81, 93
  Town development, 97

PLANNING —
  Permission, 96
  Application, 97
  Residential, 97, 98

POSSESSION *(see also VACANT)*, 33, 82, 84

PRESERVATION ORDER, 33, 130

PRICE: market, 6

PROBATE, 101, 124
  District registry, 124

RATES, 136
  General, 113, 137
  Personal debt, 137
  Water, 113, 136
  Value, 81, 91

RECEIPT: valid, 50

REGISTRATION —
  Application for, 111
  Caution against, 74
  Compulsory, 138, 143
  First (1A), 142

REGISTER of LOCAL LAND CHARGES *(see SEARCH)*

REQUISITIONS, 49, 51

RESTRICTION, 67, 68

RIGHTS, 48
  of occupation, 92, 151
  of way, 90, 126
  Public, 94

ROADS —
  Maintenance, 72
  Unmade, 72, 94, 103, 104
  Private, 132

SEALS, 139

SEARCH —
  Certificates, 125, 133
  Land Registry official search, 75, 113, 114,
  Land Registry reply, 54
      Index map, 64, 74, 128, 133, 152
  Land charges, official search, 128, 133, 144
      Bankruptcy only, 61, 96, 114
  Local land charges, 61, 96, 99, 104, 130
  District Councils, 61, 97, 98, 104, 130, 132

SERVICES (see DRAINS ELECTRICITY, GAS, WATER)

SEWER: main, 66, 72

SEWERAGE, 95

SILENCE implies consent, 17

SMOKE CONTROL, 104

SOCRATES, 35

STAGE PAYMENTS, 38

STAKEHOLDER, 12, 49, 83, 100, 106, 135, 141, 142

STAMPS
    Certificate of Value, 109, 110
    Duties, 101, 112, 140
    Land Registry, 79, 87
    Offices, 167
    Particulars delivered, 113, 119

STATE GUARANTEE, 83

STATUTORY ACKNOWLEDGEMENT, 137

STATUTORY DECLARATION, 94

SUBSIDENCE, 22

SURVEYOR —
    Chartered, 16, 19, 29, 30
    Fees, 39, 41
    Reports, 41

SURVIVOR TAKES ALL, 109, 115, 138

TAX —
    Capital transfer, 70
    Death duties, 109
    Mortgage relief, 43, 44, 45

TENANT —
    For life, 50
    Joint, 109

TITLE, ix, 49, 100ff
    Emmett on, 94
    Proving, 62
    Registration of, 62, 63
    Requisitions on 49, 83, 85, 110, 112, 113, 136, 141
    Safe custody, 137
    Squatters, 65
    State guarantee, 62

TITLE, REGISTERED —
  Absolute, 65
  Landlords, 149
  Leasehold, 65
  Number, 64, 87, 89, (new) 138
  Possessory, 65
  Requisitions on, 83

TITLE, UNREGISTERED —
  Abstract of 127, 135
  Deeds lost, 63
  Examined, 136
  Endorsed, 136
  Root of, 52, 121, 126, 132

TIMBER ROT, 26, 27

TRANSFER —
  Draft, 83, 108, 110
  Form 19: 83, 84, 108, 113, 116, 118, 120, 142
      Completing, 138
  Signing, 115

UNDERTAKING, 84, 131

VACANT POSSESSION, 33, 91, 118

VACANT PROPERTY, 84

VENDOR —
  Capacity, 4, 100, 101
  Joint Tenants, 109

WATER, 94
  Supply, 28

WILLS, 135

Also see Glossary

Glossary

Absolute title — highest and most unquestionable title.

Abstract of title — a summary of documents proving title.

Assent — the title of a legatee or devisee is not complete until the deceased's executor/personal representative has completed an assent which then becomes a good root of title.

Assignment — transfer of benefit of lease.

Attested — witnessed.

Beneficial owner — person/s owning land for own benefit.

Beneficiary — one who has the beneficial interest i.e. receives the rent or is the occupier.

Charge/legal charge — mortgage.

Counterpart — lease signed by tenant — the *part* is signed by landlord.

Conveyance — a written instrument of transfer of real property used when the land is not registered at H.M. Land Registry.

Covenant — promise written in deed.

Deed — is "signed, sealed and delivered" all transfers of freehold and leasehold property must be.

Devise — a gift by will of land or other real estate.
A *bequest* is a gift by will of personal estate.

Easement — right of one landowner to use others land for right of way, water, drains etc.

Escrow — a deed delivered conditionally, it does not become effective until the condition is satisfied e.g. other party signs his part.

Estate — (a) real: ownership of freehold/leasehold.
(b) personal: ownership of effects other than land.

Epitome of title — a list of deeds which constitute title to property.

Execute — sign.

Executor — person appointed in will of deceased person to carry out provisions of will. Probate proves entitlement to do so.

Fee simple — freehold.

Filed plan — the plan from which Land Registry identifies land.

Freehold — absolute ownership as opposed to leasehold.

Intestate — leaving no valid will.

Indenture — Deed made by more than one party. A conveyance used to be called an Indenture.

174

Joint & Several — Two or more parties who render themselves liable to a joint action against all, as well as to a separate action against each in case the agreement or bond is not kept.

Joint tenants — co-owners of land with or without buildings on it. Survivor takes all (see also — tenants in common).

Land — general real estate term, refers to land and all buildings that stand on it.

Overriding interest — The rights of persons other than owners to occupy property. These rights do not have to be registered at the Land Registry to be effective.

Parcels — The pieces a hitherto single plot has been split into.

Private Treaty — Sale not by auction.

Restrictive covenant — promise in a deed restricting use of land.

Root of title — documents through which ownership is proved. (Will become archaic when all land registered.)

Scrotage — A Bradshavian neologism.

Seisen/seised — possessed of land as freeholders.

Sitting Tenant — Tenant of house or flat. So referred to when landlord offers to sell to him or her.

Specific performance — successful completion of contract.

Stakeholder — holder of deposit which he does not pass to vendor without authority of buyer, or return to buyer without permission of vendor.

Stamp duty — payable on some deeds and documents which cannot be used as evidence or registered at the Land Registry unless properly stamped **with** duty paid, or 'adjudicated' or 'particulars delivered'.

Tenure — The mode of holding or occupying lands. No person except the Sovereign can be the absolute owner of land in England. So the rest of us hold immediately of the crown (freehold) or mediated by a freeholder (leasehold). How far a tenure extends is called the tenant's estate, hence estate in fee simple etc.

Tenant for life — person entitled to benefit of real estate for term of his life, after which it will pass to others as determined by an existing will or trust.

Testimonium — formal introduction to the attestation clause in a deed.

Title — evidence which signifies a person's right to enjoyment of land.

Trust — created when property transferred to a person (trustee) to apply for benefit of another.

Trustees for sale — Where two or more people are entitled to the estate. Purchasers need receipt for purchase monies on conveyance or Form 19 signed by at least two of them unless there are two joint tenants and only one survives. The survivor can then deal with the estate.

Vacating receipt — Receipt written and signed on the Legal Charge showing all monies intended to be secured by the deed to have been paid off.

Buying at Auction

When the hammer falls a binding contract between the last bidder and the vendor is made. Don't worry about having a bout of involuntary head nodding. The auctioneer knows the difference between a bidder and a nutter.

Follow the drill outlined below. Attend some auctions no matter what the property for sale. If it is obvious that the property is worth £30,000 and the bidding opens at £15,000 make a bid. It's exciting, it's free and you have had a dress rehearsal and prepared yourself for the real thing later.

You prepare by doing what any house buyer should do, or have done for him, before signing a contract:

1. See and approve the contract
2. Have enquiries before contract form answered
3. Have Local Authority forms completed and answered
4. Send search forms to Land Registry/Legal Charges Dept.

A vendor's solicitor should have prepared a set of the above and the Agent will have a supply. If all the replies on the forms meet with your approval so well and good. If not, ask questions until you are satisfied or lose interest. So far you haven't spent a penny... and that is how it should be. If you need a mortgage leave your enquiries about it as late as possible, others could be in the same position and some anxious soul might already have paid a survey fee to one of the local lenders who can then give you an idea of what could be borrowed. Give them all a chance of not wasting a survey fee for you.

Follow the instructions given (p.97) about actually visiting the local council offices and gleaning information that other bidders might not hear about, because their hired helps have relied on only doing the paper work. You might find out from the officials that fifty years ago there was a proposal to do something nasty in the vicinity. Ask the auctioneer if there is any likelihood of the plan being revived. He will only be able to give a vague reply. You react with a long face for all to see because you will have positioned yourself at the end of the front row where by sitting side-ways-on you can keep an eye on the whole assembly and know whether the auctioneer is getting genuine bids or taking them off the chandeliers.

Ref. p.108:

There is no set fee for this service. So, as most solicitors are authorised to act for most building societies, ring round the local Skinners for quotations before you make your mortgage application. Ask if they are on the roll of the society of your choice, say you are working out of a good conveyancing guide so won't make a nuisance of yourself, and ask for a quotation. You can then say to the society, "My solicitor friend Mr Skinner says he will act for you. I hope that will be in order." It should be. Building societies don't gladly fall out with local solicitors.

Aim to pay the recommended scale agreed between the Building Societies' Association and the Law Society:

Advance not exceeding	Scale	Advance not exceeding	Scale
£10,000	52.50	£25,000	72.50
£15,000	62.50	£30,000	75.00
£20,000	67.50	£35,000	76.25

Exceeding £35,000. Add 50p per £5,000 or part thereof.

Instalment Advances Additional £7.50 per instalment (maximum £22.50).

These charges do not include disbursements or V.A.T.

The flow diagrams assume that Mr. Feather's solicitors, Messrs Skinner, Dordle and Altman strictly divide the work between pre and post contract, not being as accommodating nor as keen to get a move on as D.I.Y. conveyancer Mr. Bold.

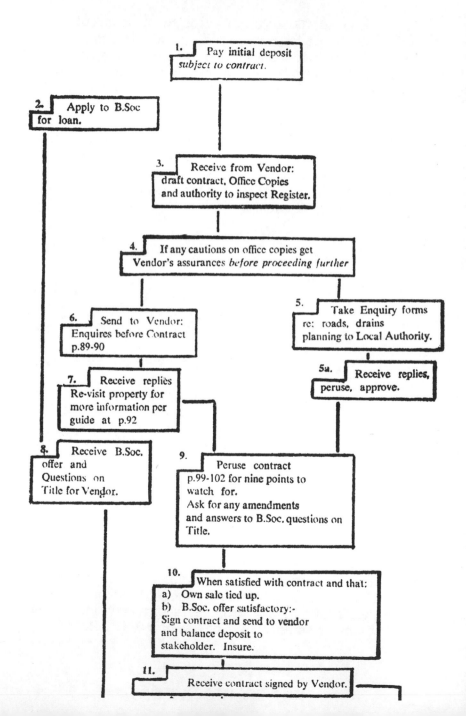

1. Pay initial deposit *subject to contract.*

2. Apply to B.Soc for loan.

3. Receive from Vendor: draft contract, Office Copies and authority to inspect Register.

4. If any cautions on office copies get Vendor's assurances *before proceeding further*

5. Take Enquiry forms re: roads, drains planning to Local Authority.

6. Send to Vendor: Enquires before Contract p.89-90

7. Receive replies Re-visit property for more information per guide at p.92

5a. Receive replies, peruse, approve.

8. Receive B.Soc. offer and Questions on Title for Vendor.

9. Peruse contract p.99-102 for nine points to watch for. Ask for any amendments and answers to B.Soc. questions on Title.

10. When satisfied with contract and that:
a) Own sale tied up.
b) B.Soc. offer satisfactory:-
Sign contract and send to vendor and balance deposit to stakeholder. Insure.

11. Receive contract signed by Vendor.

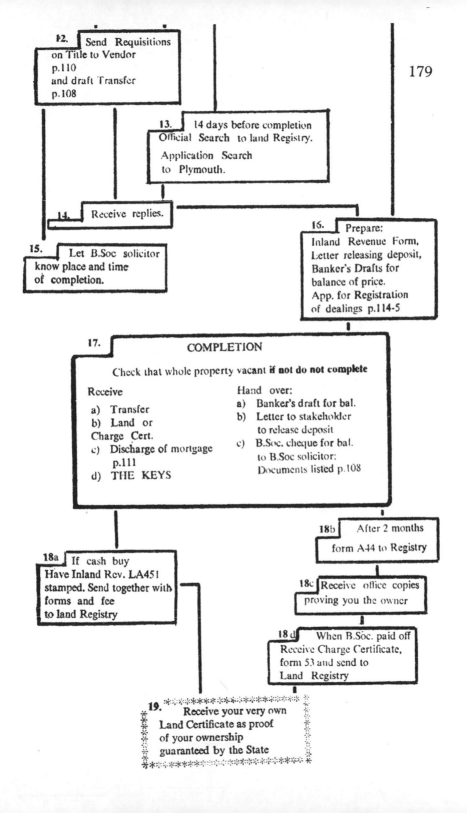

12. Send Requisitions on Title to Vendor p.110 and draft Transfer p.108

13. 14 days before completion Official Search to land Registry.
Application Search to Plymouth.

14. Receive replies.

15. Let B.Soc solicitor know place and time of completion.

16. Prepare:
Inland Revenue Form,
Letter releasing deposit,
Banker's Drafts for balance of price.
App. for Registration of dealings p.114-5

17. COMPLETION

Check that whole property vacant **if not do not complete**

Receive
a) Transfer
b) Land or Charge Cert.
c) Discharge of mortgage p.111
d) THE KEYS

Hand over:
a) Banker's draft for bal.
b) Letter to stakeholder to release deposit
c) B.Soc. cheque for bal. to B.Soc solicitor:
Documents listed p.108

18a If cash buy Have Inland Rev. LA451 stamped. Send together with forms and fee to land Registry

18b After 2 months form A44 to Registry

18c Receive office copies proving you the owner

18 d When B.Soc. paid off Receive Charge Certificate, form 53 and send to Land Registry

19. Receive your very own Land Certificate as proof of your ownership guaranteed by the State

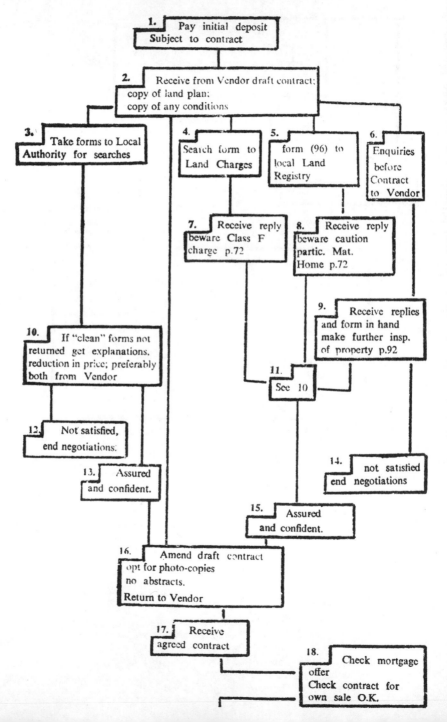

1. Pay initial deposit
Subject to contract

2. Receive from Vendor draft contract;
copy of land plan;
copy of any conditions

3. Take forms to Local
Authority for searches

4. Search form to
Land Charges

5. form (96) to
local Land
Registry

6. Enquiries
before
Contract
to Vendor

7. Receive reply
beware Class F
charge p.72

8. Receive reply
beware caution
partic. Mat.
Home p.72

9. Receive replies
and form in hand
make further insp.
of property p.92

10. If "clean" forms not
returned get explanations,
reduction in price; preferably
both from Vendor

11. See 10

12. Not satisfied,
end negotiations.

13. Assured
and confident.

14. not satisfied
end negotiations

15. Assured
and confident.

16. Amend draft contract
opt for photo-copies
no abstracts.
Return to Vendor

17. Receive
agreed contract

18. Check mortgage
offer
Check contract for
own sale O.K.

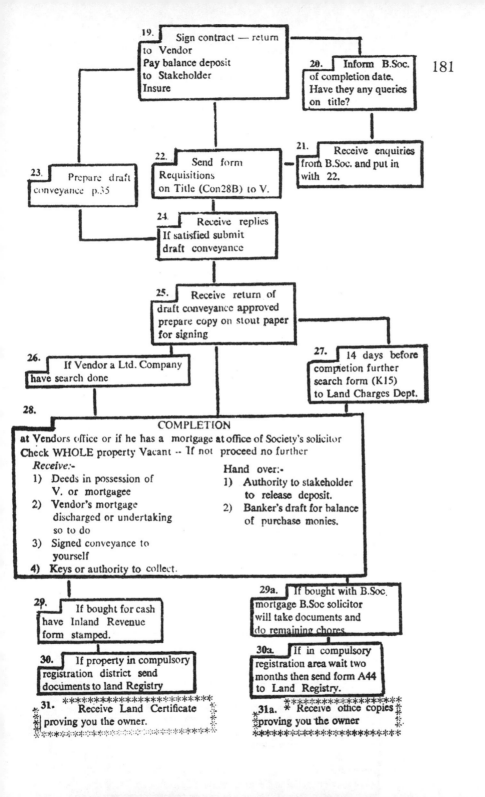

181

19. Sign contract — return to Vendor
Pay balance deposit to Stakeholder
Insure

20. Inform B.Soc. of completion date. Have they any queries on title?

21. Receive enquiries from B.Soc. and put in with 22.

22. Send form Requisitions on Title (Con28B) to V.

23. Prepare draft conveyance p.35

24. Receive replies If satisfied submit draft conveyance

25. Receive return of draft conveyance approved prepare copy on stout paper for signing

26. If Vendor a Ltd. Company have search done

27. 14 days before completion further search form (K15) to Land Charges Dept.

28. COMPLETION
at Vendors office or if he has a mortgage at office of Society's solicitor
Check WHOLE property Vacant -- If not proceed no further

Receive:-
1) Deeds in possession of V. or mortgagee
2) Vendor's mortgage discharged or undertaking so to do
3) Signed conveyance to yourself
4) Keys or authority to collect.

Hand over:-
1) Authority to stakeholder to release deposit.
2) Banker's draft for balance of purchase monies.

29. If bought for cash have Inland Revenue form stamped.

29a. If bought with B.Soc. mortgage B.Soc solicitor will take documents and do remaining chores.

30. If property in compulsory registration district send documents to land Registry

30a. If in compulsory registration area wait two months then send form A44 to Land Registry.

31. *************************
Receive Land Certificate proving you the owner.
****

31a. *************************
Receive office copies proving you the owner
****

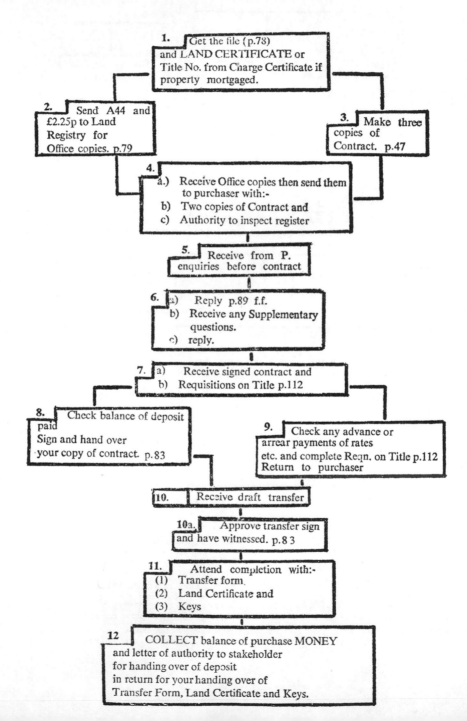

1. Get the file (p.78) and LAND CERTIFICATE or Title No. from Charge Certificate if property mortgaged.

2. Send A44 and £2.25p to Land Registry for Office copies. p.79

3. Make three copies of Contract. p.47

4.
a.) Receive Office copies then send them to purchaser with:-
b) Two copies of Contract and
c) Authority to inspect register

5. Receive from P. enquiries before contract

6.
a) Reply p.89 f.f.
b) Receive any Supplementary questions.
c) reply.

7.
a) Receive signed contract and
b) Requisitions on Title p.112

8. Check balance of deposit paid Sign and hand over your copy of contract. p.83

9. Check any advance or arrear payments of rates etc. and complete Reqn. on Title p.112 Return to purchaser

10. Receive draft transfer

10a. Approve transfer sign and have witnessed. p.83

11. Attend completion with:-
(1) Transfer form.
(2) Land Certificate and
(3) Keys

12 COLLECT balance of purchase MONEY and letter of authority to stakeholder for handing over of deposit in return for your handing over of Transfer Form, Land Certificate and Keys.

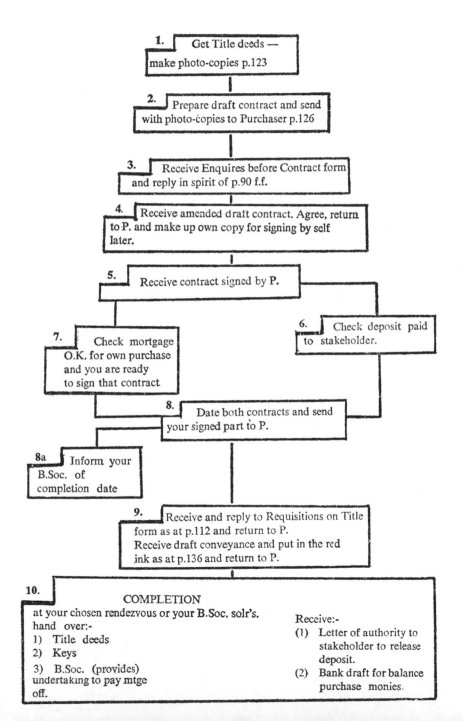

1. Get Title deeds — make photo-copies p.123

2. Prepare draft contract and send with photo-copies to Purchaser p.126

3. Receive Enquires before Contract form and reply in spirit of p.90 f.f.

4. Receive amended draft contract. Agree, return to P. and make up own copy for signing by self later.

5. Receive contract signed by P.

6. Check deposit paid to stakeholder.

7. Check mortgage O.K. for own purchase and you are ready to sign that contract

8. Date both contracts and send your signed part to P.

8a Inform your B.Soc. of completion date

9. Receive and reply to Requisitions on Title form as at p.112 and return to P.
Receive draft conveyance and put in the red ink as at p.136 and return to P.

10. COMPLETION
at your chosen rendezvous or your B.Soc. solr's.
hand over:-
1) Title deeds
2) Keys
3) B.Soc. (provides) undertaking to pay mtge off.

Receive:-
(1) Letter of authority to stakeholder to release deposit.
(2) Bank draft for balance purchase monies.

Bradshaw's Guide to Marketing Your House

If you are thinking of selling your house without an estate agent this book gives you detailed inside information on how to beat the system and save up to £1,000. How to window-dress your house, write particulars, keep prospects keen; how to do no-deposit-no-legal-fee schemes; bargaining: what ploys to use. Why D.I.Y. vendors win.

ISBN 0 950 7170 4 5   Paperback   £2.50

Bradshaw's Guide to House Conveyancing for Sitting Tenants

Special conveyancing procedures have been agreed between the Government and the Land Registry for council and other tenants who now have the right to buy their homes. £150 or more can be saved by following these simple instructions and check lists to buy the house that you already live in.

ISBN 0 9507170 1 0   Paperback   £2.50

Bradshaw's Guide to Conveyancing by Way of Gift and Inheritance

How to put an extra name(s) on your deeds or take one off without going to a solicitor. Doing it now could save a lot of trouble later. Easy-to-follow instructions for conveyances where no money passes, — basically a quick and simple job — once you know how.

ISBN 0 9507170 2 9   Paperback   £5.00

To: **Castle Books, 1 Blackdown, Leamington Spa, CV32 6RA**

please supply:

Bradshaw's Guide to Conveyancing by Way of Gift or Inheritance	5.50	
Bradshaw's Guide to DIY House Buying, Selling and Conveyancing – 2nd Edition. paperback	5.45	
hardcover	8.45	
Bradshaw's Guide to Conveyancing for Sitting Tenants.	3.00	
Bradshaw's Guide to Marketing your House (selling without an Estate Agent)	3.00	
Total enclosed:		£

All prices include postage and packing.
Please enclose cash, postal order or cheque with order.

Name..

Address ....